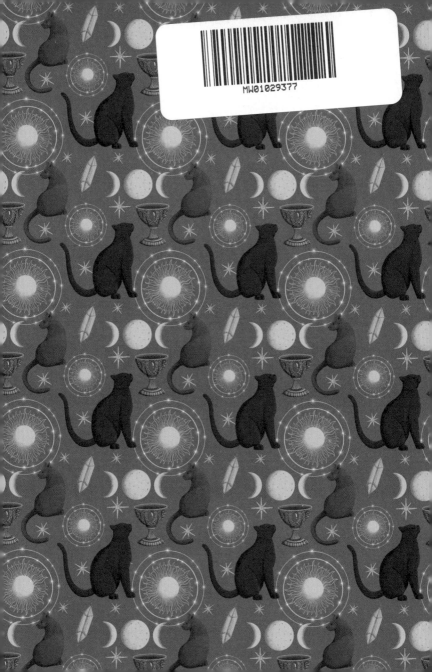

CAT GODS, GODDESSES, DEITIES, AND DEMONS

A Guide to Feline Folklore and Mythology

NATALIE BOVIS

ILLUSTRATED BY LUCY ROSE

Running Press

PHILADELPHIA

Running Press
Hachette Book Group
1290 Avenue of the Americas, New York, NY 10104
www.runningpress.com
@Running_Press

First Edition: April 2025

Published by Running Press, an imprint of Hachette Book Group, Inc.
The Running Press name and logo are trademarks of Hachette Book Group, Inc.

The Hachette Speakers Bureau provides a wide range of authors for speaking events. To find out more, go to www.hachettespeakersbureau.com or email HachetteSpeakers@hbgusa.com.

Running Press books may be purchased in bulk for business, educational, or promotional use. For more information, please contact your local bookseller or the Hachette Book Group Special Markets Department at Special.Markets@hbgusa.com.

The publisher is not responsible for websites (or their content) that are not owned by the publisher.

Print book cover and interior design by Jenna McBride

Library of Congress Cataloging-in-Publication Data has been applied for.

ISBNs: 978-0-7624-8801-8 (hardcover), 978-0-7624-8802-5 (ebook)

Printed in China

1010

10 9 8 7 6 5 4 3 2 1

For all who protect animals, the Earth,
and the sacred, wild spaces

"In ancient times, cats were worshipped as gods;
they have not forgotten this."

—TERRY PRATCHETT

CONTENTS

· · · · · · · · · ·

INTRODUCTION

Cat lovers may see a kitten as nature's most perfect creature with its exquisite combination of innocence, fragility, and emerging agility. Lolling in the sun, purring beneath a caress, and tracking all movement with their ever-curious gaze, they are magical—and adorable—little bundles of Divine Feline Energy. On the other end of the fantastic feline spectrum, a grown male lion's magnificence inspires awe, love, fear, and more tales than we can count. Large or small, tamed or fierce, throughout the history of humanity, cats have played a sacred role in our lives, from beloved pet to revered deity.

Evidence of the special connection between cats and people is unceasing. Archeologists have found cat remains buried with humans as far back as the tenth millennium BCE in Cyprus, and the Greek goddess Hecate is said to have regularly assumed the form of a cat. Hieroglyphics tell us that ancient Egyptians worshipped cat gods, and their queen Cleopatra had a kitty companion in her palace whom she named Tivali. Among the many feline Egyptian deities, Bastet and Sekhmet are the most well-known, and depicted with women's bodies and the heads of a cat and a lion, respectively. They each had their own cults and temples, and to this day, people place offerings for them on their home altars.

A Chinese cat goddess called Li Shou is said to have protected farmers from mice, and Ai Apaec was a pre-Inca god with fangs and whiskers whose image descended from an even more ancient cat god. The Hindu goddess Durga represents feminine power and rides atop an enchanted lion. Similarly, a Semitic goddess known as Asherah or Qadesh was referred to as the Lion Lady. Magical cats have been revered through millennia and are not only from far-flung places in centuries past. In modern-day Washington, DC, rumored sightings of the so-called Demon Cat slinking around the White House persist.

This book is more than a guide to ancient cat gods. It is an exploration of the way humans have observed, interacted with, learned from, and revered Mother Nature and her wild children. Whether two-legged, four-legged, feathered, scaled, or finned, the other beings sharing the planet with us were sacred to our ancestors who understood that all life is interconnected. The very universal energy that powers the sun and stars makes trees grow and ocean tides swell, and it runs through the physical bodies of every creature that has ever lived. Some people call this life force a *soul* and cat god worshippers may refer to it as Divine Feline Energy.

Ancient folklore is rife with examples of animal cunning and compassion, and many humans invoked other species as spiritual guides. Some took that a step further and flat out worshipped them as gods. Animism is the worship of animals, or animallike gods, and felinism brings that focus to cats. Arguably, cats are the most intriguing of animals because of how deeply we relate to them. Much like us, they are free spirits and adaptable survivors. We admire them for their dignity, independence, and ferocity. They are clever hunters and stealthy wanderers. Sometimes, vulnerable feral mother cats with kittens band together in cat colonies. When tending to their young, cats are gentle nurturers who guide their babies to become self-sufficient. They are also unrelenting protectors against an intruder who might cause harm. Aren't these just the sort of qualities we mortals wish for in a god?

Cats are majestic and full of contradiction. Their expressive faces can portray a curious baby doll with eyes darting from dangling string to fluffy toy mouse, or that of a concentrating and ruthless hunter. Their soft fur and lithe bodies take on molten shapes when they are at rest or lounging with their young. Then, in a flash, from nose to tail, they transform into sharp edges as their taut muscles draw into bowstrings ready to spring forth. Eyes narrow, claws outstretch, lips draw back with fangs at the ready . . . and pounce! Whether a cuddly house cat, an apex predator in pursuit of a deer flashing across an African savannah, or a jaguar camouflaged in an Amazonian rainforest, everything about these beings is otherworldly, mysterious, and slightly unpredictable. No wonder they fascinate us.

As you explore the cat gods in this book, you will meet the feline deities and demons from civilizations around the globe. You'll also encounter mystical cats who work in alliance with human gods and goddesses. The feline entities on the following pages come from different eras and cultures. Some are angelic guides, and others, demonic adversaries, but all play a role in our understanding of feline deities and why they were elevated to god like status. Ultimately, the way people worship tells us a lot about humanity, past and present.

For millennia, Indigenous people have ritualized calling upon the Divine Feline Energy emanating from cat gods. And, when discussing cat deities, Ancient Egypt is the first place that comes to mind. Cats in the Arabic world are still widely respected as clean animals who carry good fortune, and so they have been allowed into mosques and other holy spaces. Many Greek and Roman gods and goddesses worked in conjunction with cats, were depicted with feline heads, or were transformed into cats themselves. People across Asian countries and the Americas also share tales of mythological cat beings, and in these areas we find dark depictions of cat demons. Modern European societies also run the gamut from kindly stories of cats saving the day to gruesome tales encouraging children to beware of feline monsters.

With such a range of cat gods, goddesses, deities, and demons, and a mind-boggling expanse of human mysticism to explore, spanning millennia and continents, the magical cats in this book are grouped into four geographical families: Africa, the Americas, Asia, and Europe. There is some overlap, of course, but by dividing them up in this way we can begin to consider this fascinating subject. The South Pacific, Australia, and New Zealand are not well represented here, because cats were not native to those regions so they are elusive in ancient tales.

Cats did not roam the shores "down under" until they arrived on ships with people from other parts of the world, with the first recorded cat sightings in the 1700s. Cats sailed with explorers, pirates, and conquerors alike to kill stowaway rodents that might eat the food brought on board for the sailors. Once on land, these working cats snuck off the ships and gained their own freedom. This means that prior to oceanic exploration, the ancient people in some parts of the globe did not have the opportunity to observe the marvels of felines, so they don't appear in ancient worship. Today, though, we can be sure that cat lovers exist in every corner of the world.

If you are holding this book, you evidently have an interest in cats and their influence on ancient spirituality, so I hope you will surrender to wonder as you thumb through the pages. When learning about these creatures, you may become inspired to incorporate Divine Feline Energy into your own life. We have much to learn from cats in both their physical form and mystical incarnations. Clearly, the people who lived upon the Earth before we got here thought so.

Although some people around the world still engage in felinism, lionism, and other forms of cat worship, the spread of Christianity, Islam, and other modern monotheistic religions largely put an end to animal reverence. Sadly, under most religions, animals are not only disregarded but seen as mere commodities or beasts of burden. Since the industrial revolution, animal suffering under humans has reached horrifying depths. As animal advocates, we must extol the value of animals as sentient beings rather than normalizing the pain people continue to inflict upon them.

In recent years, modern forms of cat worship have emerged. Social media is overflowing with cat memes, kitten videos, and accounts curated by celebrity kitties and their humans. These popular online communities are not only fun playgrounds for those of us obsessed with the adorable nature of cats, but they also translate to big business by way of paid endorsements and advertising for the content creators.

The first major Cat Show, or gathering of cat devotees, was held at the Crystal Palace in London in 1871 and at Madison Square Garden in New York in 1895. Today's cat cafés are also a testament to our love for feline friends. Even if someone cannot take home a kitty of their own, they can enjoy a cup of tea with an adoptable pal for a couple of hours. While these cafés started in Asia, they are now a global phenomenon. In a stressful world, people long for the kind of tactile comfort only a cat can provide.

In various energy healing practices around the world, some people also believe in absorbing good vibes from other living, and nonliving, sources. This is exemplified by filling one's home with plants to filter the air or hiring a feng shui expert to create a harmonious flow within a room by reordering the furniture. The cat people of the world will attest to the unique abilities of cats to protect us against negative feelings by simply sharing space with us. Their soothing purrs, warm cuddles, and amusing playfulness evoke smiles and provide endless fodder for kitty-centric joy. Charles Dickens, Mark Twain, William Wordsworth, John Keats, Thomas Hardy, Lewis Carol, C. S. Lewis, Freddie Mercury, Ernest Hemingway, Taylor Swift, and Ricky Gervais are only a handful of celebrated writers and artists who have professed their love of felines and exalted them in poems, songs, paintings, and stories.

Peeking behind the curtain of cat worship will also help you get to know your own pet cat in a more meaningful way. I hope that by learning about the cat gods on the following pages it will intrigue you to tap into your own Divine Feline Energy. If you want to go a step further and communicate with these cat gods regularly, you can pull messages from the *Cat Gods, Goddesses, Deities, and Demons Oracle Deck and Guidebook*, which serves as a companion to this anthology.

Note: The cat gods, goddesses, deities, and demons in this book are shared with the intention to celebrate the Divine Feline Energy flowing throughout human cultures. It is acknowledged that much of the following material has roots in Indigenous societies and it is put forth, respectfully, as a compilation of information to make it easier for cat lovers to learn about magical felines and the people whose traditions highlight cats in their mysticism.

AFRICA

Africa is considered the cradle of humanity, and evolutionary science tells us that it is where two-legged, upright-walking, verbal-communicating, group-living mammals originated. But beyond the challenge of daily survival, what moved those early humans? Did they live a spiritual life? Archeological evidence tells us they did. So where did the concept of a god originate?

As our species evolved to have a curious mind, early humans sought to explain the world around them while nearly everything happening was out of their control. By finding reasons for the way things worked or why they occurred, perhaps we could gain some autonomy. Creating a relationship with spiritual guides and gods who connect us with a power larger than themselves was an attractive idea and remains so today.

Believing in a god or gods who control what is happening in the world helps people feel that there is order in the chaos. It would be convenient to ask a god for help with the challenges we face in life. Is it possible that other species who roam the planet with humans are reflections of such gods?

Before the great dispersal of humans by mass migration around the globe some fifty thousand years ago, the very concept of spirituality—or the desire to understand the world through stories—would be continually reshaped as the wandering groups encountered native populations with their own unique customs. Their old beliefs were challenged as they came upon previously unknown lands, observed others' rituals surrounding the cycle of life from birth to death, and became fascinated with the inherent gifts displayed by fellow creatures. Animals remained central figures in ever-evolving cultures, everywhere.

Humans are born helpless and require years of assistance before we can feed ourselves, find shelter, and navigate community hierarchies on our own, so we admire the superiority of other species' abilities to survive independently from an early age. Sure, sometimes people hunted their fellow wildlings, and sometimes people were the ones hunted, but that's a somewhat fair exchange in the animal kingdom, isn't it? The interconnectedness of humans with other animals eventually led to some mutually beneficial partnerships, too, such as the domestication of dogs and cats. Well, if one can ever consider a cat truly domesticated.

It is believed that cats first became members of our families around ten thousand years ago although, admittedly, there are few physical remains to prove this. That said, the archeologist Alain Le Brun discovered a carefully buried cat skeleton on the island of Cyprus dating to around 9500 BCE. This is significant because cats were not indigenous to that little strip of land, so it means that someone brought their kitty there, raised it, and honored it in death.

We have overwhelming evidence of the incorporation of cats into human society about 3,500 years ago by the Egyptians. One excavated feline skeleton shows healed bone fractures, which suggests it was cared for by a human, almost certainly as a household pet. Cats flourished in ancient Egypt because they were offered food and shelter and often exalted to godlike status. Their descendants are the domesticated cats we still adore, in all corners of the world. As a matter of fact, the very word *cat* likely comes from the North African word *quattah*, further demonstrating how early peoples' associations with cats continue to impact us today.

Upon discovering the tombs of ancient Egyptian rulers, explorers and plunderers came upon piles of golden treasures. Among the sarcophagi, amulets, and instructions on how to enter the afterlife written in hieroglyphics, there were sometimes skeletal remains of human servants entombed with these higher-ranked people. There were shimmering and bejeweled statues of various gods, including the cat deities as well as mummified cats, which is where we get the idea that these animals were respected, feared, loved, and—quite literally—worshipped.

At that time, people were mummified to preserve their bodies so that their spirits would be contained rather than lost in the ether of dusty air inside a pyramid or other such tomb. Many mummies of animals valued by Egyptians have been found in these tombs, such as snakes, dogs, bulls, and, of course, thousands upon thousands of cats.

The process of mummifying cost both money and time, so only pharaohs, queens, and members of the noble class got this special treatment. We can therefore assume that the animals who were preserved in this way were of great importance. Did the people believe that these animals had souls in need of protection, too? Were these cats thought to be as holy as the god-like human leaders of their day? From this we can conclude yes.

Animism was widespread throughout the early advanced civilizations. Ancient Thebes, whose ruins lay in modern-day Luxor, was the capital of Egypt around 2000 BCE. Its holy triad of deities consisted of Amun-Re along with his consort goddess Mut, the Great Mother, who was a maternal goddess often depicted with a lion's head. Her son Khonsu, who personified the moon, rounded out that threesome.

In 334 BCE, Alexander the Great marched forth from Greece through Europe and into India, conquering Egypt along the way. At the time, Thebes stood as a striking testimony to Egyptian civilization with its colorful temples and ornate palaces, the necropolises of the Valley of the Kings and the Valley of the Queens, the pyramids, and the Great Sphinx. It is believed that he was so impressed by the monuments that he let them stand instead of tearing them down, which would have further subjugated the conquered.

Rather than eliminating the Egyptian gods and goddesses as his Greek people settled the area and formed the Ptolemaic dynasty, they incorporated them into their own mythology. For example, Bastet—the most well-known Egyptian cat deity—was melded with the Greek goddess Artemis, who took the form of a sultry feline at times. Felinism flourished throughout the area, even spreading back to Greece, where the Greek city of Leontopolis became home to several lion god-worshipping cults.

A few centuries later, around 30 BCE, the Roman emperor Octavian, later known as Augustus, famously took control of Egypt when he ousted Mark Antony and Cleopatra in the Battle of Actium. With this conquest, many Egyptian and Greek gods merged with Roman gods. Diana, the Roman Goddess of the Hunt, was seen as having catlike qualities, which made her the easy replacement for Bastet and Artemis.

Underground worshippers of Bastet remained, and some of them brought her cult back to the area we now recognize as Italy. Traces of Bastet's devotees, such as ancient cat amulets, have been discovered in Rome and Pompeii. Ultimately, the convergence of these powerful cultures and polytheistic religions leads to some repetition of the cat gods on the following pages whereby a goddess known by one name by one particular group is reminiscent of a goddess in another era.

On record, though, Egypt was the first powerful civilization with evidence of cat veneration dating back to 4000 BCE, where felinism was particularly tied to fertility, nobility, and war. Those early cat gods were strongly associated with the sun god of creation, Ra, who was said to take the form of a cat himself when fighting the evil serpent demon Apophis or Apep of the Underworld at night before his victorious return at dawn each day.

Most of the Egyptian cat gods are shape-shifters or hybrid creatures with a human body and a wildcat head. The famed sphinx is the opposite with a lion's body, eagle wings, and watchful eyes in its human head. This melding of cat and person symbolizes how enmeshed the people felt with felines.

In the early Egyptian eras, it was also believed that a god could enter the body of any living human or animal. This period saw the rise of cat goddess cults, because once believed to be the incarnation of a god, that mortal being could then give oracles, be prayed to, and receive offerings. Upon the death of that human or animal body, the god would leave that flesh casing and enter another. This is an early version of reincarnation that was popularized in later Far Eastern belief systems such as Buddhism. Once relieved of the Divine Feline Energy that had inhabited it, the body was then mummified and entombed in a temple or other sacred place.

Carved feline statuettes and cat mummies became extremely popular and were even sold and traded among individuals. Whether in homes or in communal worship, people knelt before these religious icons to pray for favors or give gratitude to their favorite cat deity. A feline corpse preserved by mummification was such a popular offering that those who did not have the means to obtain one of their own created fake kitty mummies to leave as gifts to the gods.

Throughout the early civilizations, cat colonies were beneficial because they kept rodents and venomous vipers at bay. It was even against Egyptian law to harm a cat. One tale speaks of a Roman soldier who was murdered by an angry mob when he accidentally killed a kitten. Cats who were considered holy—sometimes even lions—were bred within the temples.

Kindness to cats is a long-honored tradition in Arabic cultures. As recent as the last century, street cats were fed daily in the gardens of the high court of Cairo. This ritual had been in place since the 1200s when the Mamluk sultan al-Zahir Baybars, a cat lover himself, decreed the space a cat garden. Over time, the place changed hands, but the monarch's law continued to be carried out.

The Persian tale of the great hero Rostam recounts the origin of cats as an act of divine gratitude. While riding his horse one day, he saved a wandering magician from being killed by a band of thieves. That night, the magician asked him what he would like in return for his good deed. Rostam humbly proclaimed that he already had all he needed with the warm fire before them and beautiful night sky above.

The magician was not satisfied with that answer, so he encapsulated a handful of smoke from above the flames, brought down the two brightest stars, and said the spell of creation over them. From the plumes of smoke emerged the most adorable gray kitten with bright yellow eyes. This new furry friend greatly pleased Rostam and he treasured the cat for the rest of its life.

It is interesting to note that most leonine deities in the early North African cultures are female, considering that these were male-dominated cultures. Relating a beautiful woman with the most ferocious predator might seem contradictory. Why were they not male?

Quite possibly this association with feminine power and the savage maternal instinct to protect one's offspring or spiritual devotees can be traced back to Ishtar, a goddess in early Mesopotamia, modern-day Iraq, who held unparalleled power and was often depicted as a lioness. Among the pantheon of Anunnaki gods, she was a fierce warrior and the goddess of sexual pleasure. Before Ishtar, Inanna was the Sumerian goddess of sensuality and battle, and after Ishtar, the Greek goddess Aphrodite took that role. All three goddesses have been associated with the planet Venus. Perhaps the elusive and uncontrollable power of love and sexual desire, the elixir of which has led many men to fight, only made sense if embodied by a female goddess, particularly one embodying the magnetism and ferocity of a lion.

In other traditional African cultures, animals also had an important place in spiritual practices, royal leadership, health, and cultural identity. They were considered divine messengers with omens coming directly from the gods, and sometimes the animals were seen as gods themselves. Animal totems and symbols played key roles in forming relationships with individuals within one's own clan and with outsiders. The dwindling populations of African animals, including the big cats who roamed freely across the savannahs, jungles, deserts, and forests spanning the continent, has severe impacts on not only our planet's wellness and local ecosystems but on the native people's own identities, even today.

Lions were royal members of the Shonan communities in Zimbabwe. The majestic cats served as mediums for their ancestors who were considered guardians of the land. A lion sighting held deep importance because it meant that the ancestors were visiting. It was also reassuring because the spiritual lion guardians were protecting the land and the people upon it. Therefore, it was understood that harming a lion would bring suffering to the offender and endanger the rest of their community.

Likewise, leopards were and still are revered as royal animals. They are protected today more than ever because their population is severely endangered. Killing one is deeply taboo and brings shame upon the family of anyone who harms it. In years past, the holiest of healers and highest-ranked leaders could wear a leopard skin in sacred ceremonies. Special permission would be granted on the rare occasion that a leopard could be hunted for that purpose. However, unfortunately, with humans encroaching on wild spaces, all wildcats face extinction by local farmers when the big cats feast on their livestock. Sadly, there are also still some people who visit Africa with the intention to hunt endangered animals, posing a terrible threat to their already at-risk populations.

In western Africa, particularly in Nigeria, Togo, and Benin, the Yoruba people developed a religion that blended myths, legends, proverbs, and songs. Theirs has similarities to Far Eastern philosophies in that they believe in reincarnation, destiny, and a Nirvana-like state of enlightenment known as Olodumare or becoming one with the Creator or Universal Energy. For those practicing felinism, that could also be called

Divine Feline Energy. The concept of Ashe is just such intelligent energy flowing through gods, people, animals, rain, rivers, and land alike. In their creation story, among the first creatures brought to life was a cat, once again demonstrating the importance of felines to the peoples native to the area.

In Nigeria, some religious groups believe that humans can morph into cats with the help of magic charms. Indeed, what an amazing power that would be! Naturally, this sort of witchcraft evokes fear in others, so many who still follow this line of magical practice are persecuted. Ironically, people who completely dismiss the idea of supernatural powers are ridiculed and outcast because mysticism is an important element in many old African religions.

The Bataung people are a modern Bantu tribe from the ancient Sotho-Tswana or Basotho nations who have been living in central Africa as far back as the fifth century. They then spread to eastern and southern parts of the continent, and many live in South Africa today. The word *tau* means "lion" in the Sotho-Tswana language, and their tribal name, *Bataung*, translates to "the place of the lion" or "the people of the lion's den." As one might guess, the lion is their sacred symbol. In likeness to their totem, the Bataung are considered strong warriors and excellent military strategists to this day. Among the other tribes are the Basia, who identify with the cat, and the Batlokwa, who consider their symbol the broad term "wildcat."

AKONGO

Akongo was a supreme and elegant cat god appearing in Congolese tales. Long and lean with a silky coat and soft step he was known as a benevolent deity who also had a cat's infinite curiosity. He had been observing people from afar while living in his heavenly realm and thought them to be a bit naive, but he also saw humans as somewhat infantile so he developed an affection for them. He saw their potential in the way that we look upon babies—helpless but with a capacity to learn, develop wisdom, and do great things over time. This paternal love drew him to them.

Much like the feline fur babies we know and love, when Akongo became intrigued by something, he felt a strong desire to move in for a closer look, so he came to live on Earth with the people he had been studying. However, once he witnessed people up close, he was dismayed. He heard their petty bickering and was shocked by their selfishness. He was horrified by their violence toward one another and cruelty toward the other animals that walked the Earth.

The humans' obnoxious behavior, drunkenness, and debauchery displeased Akongo and he became more disgusted each day. These were not ignorant neophytes—they chose to be ignorant and mean-spirited. Soon, he was fed up and had seen enough. With a flick of his tail, he turned away from the mayhem and disappeared into the jungle to live among the other wiser animals.

Sure, Akongo may have been judgmental of humans, but was he wrong? Perhaps a lesson we can take from his legend is that humility, generosity, and kindness are pleasing to the gods. This lesson is taught in all modern religions that people follow today. As we know, being entitled or intentionally cruel leads to being shunned and left out of social groups. Appreciating the good in family members, coworkers, and friends will create harmony and attract more good energy to us. Meanwhile, being a gossip or causing harm to others will scare away more than feline deities.

APEDEMAK

· · · · · · · · · ·

This god of war was considered to be as fierce as a lion and was often depicted as one himself. He was also sometimes represented as a human with a lion head or a lion-headed cobra. All three of these characterizations of Apedemak appear on the remaining walls of the Lion Temple erected in the first century in the royal city of Naga, or Naqa, in modern-day Sudan.

The temple was commissioned in the deity's honor by King Natakamani and Queen Amanitore, the rulers of the ancient kingdom of Nubia. The king and queen appear on each side of the entrance at the Lion Temple in vivid scenes, whereby the two thirty-six-foot-high figures tower above prisoners who are kneeling in submission. Apedemak appears as a lion between the feet of the king, ready to devour the victims of war, while smaller lions are shown attacking the people from all sides. The royal couple hold weapons, preparing to deliver fatal blows upon the unfortunate captives, as a falcon and a vulture circle the scene, a macabre symbol of the violence and death happening below them.

Descendants of the Nubians still refer to themselves as such two thousand years later. Their ancestors borrowed much from the Egyptians, including many of their gods and their reverence for cats. The god Apedemak, however, is exclusive to Nubia, often depicted carrying a bow, a sign of his warrior status.

Naqa was an important center for trade and political rule. People converged there for markets and religious festivals, so the Lion Temple, which was probably painted in bright colors at the time, would have been a spectacular gathering place for the farmers, herders, merchants, families, and priests who had traveled from miles around. There are remains of smaller temples and shrines in the area that accommodated the caravans of travelers, many coming to worship their lion god.

This god can be a symbol of alliances. While he was a lion god in his own right, his association with the king and queen elevated his visibility and status. It is said that we become a reflection of the people we most associate with, so choosing friends, colleagues, and lovers who reflect our values, passions, and personal ambitions help to highlight the qualities we most want to develop in ourselves.

BASTET

Bastet (Bast) is the most powerful and most widely known Egyptian cat goddess. She is the daughter of the sun god Ra, sister of Sekhmet (also a powerful cat deity), the consort of Ptah, and the mother of Mahees. She is the predecessor of the Greek Artemis and the Roman Diana, both of whom are goddesses of the hunt. Early accounts of Bastet describe her as an ardent, wild lioness prowling the southern desert under unforgiving and interminable heat.

Because Bastet has been around for so long and revered by so many different groups, she may also be the most contradictory Egyptian deity. It is believed that her cult originated around 3000 BCE in Saqqara. There, on the pyramid of Djoser, she is depicted with a lion's head, and was said to have an equally ferocious nature. She would wreak havoc in both heavens and Earth when angered. However, the people believed that she could be tamed with music, dance, and alcohol. Was she merely a misunderstood—though unpredictable—wild child, pleasure-seeking goddess?

By 1500 BCE, domesticated cats had become popular family members as depicted in tomb paintings found on ancient ruins. That was when Bastet's image transformed to that of a svelte woman with the head of a cat. With this new, friendlier kitty version of the goddess came a gentler persona, she was associated with fertility, sex, and revelry, and often dressed in a white flowing gown. She was a protector of pregnant women and sometimes shown to have multiple breasts reflecting cats' fertility.

Bastet's next robust cult was formed in the eastern delta in lower Egypt. Cat cemeteries have been uncovered at sites in both Memphis and Bubastis, and many of their bodies had been mummified. Explorers also unearthed thousands of statuettes of the cat-headed goddess within these burial sites. Many of her followers wore small cat carvings and kitty-shaped metal pendants in her honor, often buried with them around their necks, hoping to be greeted by the goddess in the next lifetime.

Over the next millennium, Bastet's cults expanded throughout Egypt. Temples in her honor sprung up in Alexandria and spread into the Mediterranean regions. During all these years, perhaps lending to her popularity, Bastet did not lose her party girl image. She sometimes appeared in brightly colored drawings carrying a sistrum (musical instrument), and festivals in her honor drew rowdy crowds from miles around. They arrived in caravans over land and came by sea on what can be regarded as early "booze cruises." The revelers brought rattles, sang loudly, and clapped their hands in joyous debauchery. Once they arrived at Bubastis, sacrifices were made, wine was guzzled, and orgiastic celebrations continued well into the night.

These parties could be considered human reenactments of cats' bawdy behavior during mating season—fertile, loud, and stopping at nothing to fulfill their biological desires. These frenzied gatherings would have pleased Bastet along with the other feline goddesses, particularly those who are identified with lionesses such as Sekhmet, Mut, and Hathor.

When seeking our deepest desires, the Divine Feline Energy of Bastet is a potent elixir. Godliness flows through each of us and our creative pursuits, and honoring it brings about profound pleasure. Whether taking a new lover, building a business, or constructing a whole new life, Bastet is the cat goddess to bring these desires to fruition.

HATHOR

• • • • • • • • •

This deity is identified as the mother of Horus, who was the god of the sky. Horus was sometimes known as the great sun god Ra who fathered many feline gods and goddesses, although further historical research explains that Horus and Ra were likely similar but separate entities. Hathor is also the goddess of sensuality, merriment, beauty, and even makeup. Sometimes she is depicted wearing horns and holding a sun disc, and at other times she is shown as a lioness. People from all classes brought her offerings in both public temples and home altars across Egypt and Nubia, an area in northeastern Africa spreading toward Libya.

An ancient goddess, even as ancient goddesses go, there is evidence that Hathor was absorbed into newer deities over time. For example, she was more or less rolled into the identity of Isis, who was embraced by the Greek and Roman populations as the mother of the gods, and we could say that all the pursuant lioness gods are incarnations of Hathor. Nubians, however, continued to recognize Hathor herself even as new cultures infiltrated Egypt over the centuries.

She was also referred to as the mother of the pharaohs and had many temples dedicated to her, including one built by Queen Tiye in the fourteenth century BCE. She also appears to be the mother of all ancient rave-like festivals in honor of feline deities. Drawings and carvings on the Temple of Philae showed people lighting torches and playing instruments and depicted jewel-clad women dancing wildly and flashing their genitals at the crowd.

While the latter activity would not be deemed appropriate today, singing, dancing, and raucous revelry is still part of many celebrations in various spiritual practices with ancient roots. At least some remnants of these wild parties exist in modern countries. In places as far away as New Orleans, women flash their breasts for Carnival beads during Mardi Gras, for example. Today's Lenten parties don't mention Hathor or other cat goddesses, but the practice of showing one's body in hedonistic partying is not entirely lost.

It is intriguing to note that historians have found some aspects of Hathor's iconography embraced by Black communities who are reclaiming their ties to African spirituality. Wearing golden arm bands and dark eyeliner, tribal dancing, and adorning oneself with many beaded necklaces can be related to early worship of this powerful and sensual goddess. Celebrating the physicality of our own womanliness and feminine freedom is a sign of the cat goddess Hathor, and her Divine Feline Energy is still flowing through us all.

MAAHES

This male lion-headed Egyptian god of war is the son of Bastet and Ptah. In some instances, he was referred to as Sekhmet's son because both sister goddesses had been portrayed with lion heads at different points in history, causing confusion among feline deity worshippers. In later centuries, Bastet's image changed to having a cat's head, which helped to differentiate the two. Maahes was also sometimes mixed up with his first cousin, Nefertem, Sekhmet's actual son, who was occasionally depicted wearing a blue lotus flower on his head and sometimes as another lion-headed male god. Still, further befuddlement came from Maahes's many nicknames, including Mihos and Mysis.

Maahes was part of the royal sun god bloodline, and as the grandson of Ra, who was the champion of the light, he was called upon to help fight the enemies such as the serpent god Apep in the dark Underworld. He is sometimes credited with helping to banish Osiris, a green-skinned god of darkness. As a protector of the pharaoh, he was usually shown carrying a knife or a sword, and so he held the moniker Lord of the Massacre.

Like his mother, Bastet, he was also associated with the scorching heat of the desert. Later in history, the Greeks who settled in Egypt considered him the maker of great storms. However, Maahes also had a kind of Robin Hood persona whereby his wrath was understood to be directed upon those who harmed the innocent and powerless, earning him yet another nickname, Avenger of Wrongs. In prayer, he is invoked to bring forth the truth in a matter.

Maahes's cult was based in the city of Leontopolis, where tamed lions were cared for and fed in the temple in his honor and that of the many feline deities. Maahes is also one of the gods depicted on the walls of the Temple of Debod, which was donated by Egypt to Spain in the 1970s. At that time, it was moved stone by stone to the Montaña Park in Madrid in order to save it from being destroyed by floods after the Aswan Dam was built. It opened to the public in 1972 and guests can still visit it in the park today.

Maahes is associated with perfumes and holy oils and considered the guardian of sacred spaces. He is the magical god of midsummer when the sun stays long in the sky, illuminating the Earth with his happiness. Nightlong feasts were held in his honor, which might also imply that, like his mother and aunt, Maahes is pleased by his devotees eating, drinking, and making merriment.

One of the takeaways from Maahes's legend is finding our purpose in life through both inner and outward satisfaction. Enjoying the pleasurable aspects of our bodies and spiritual exploration is important to happiness. So, too, is finding a cause beyond us and, like Maahes, becoming avengers of wrongs in the world. Everyone has the power to help those who are powerless, voiceless, and abused. Many spiritual practices put forth the idea that helping others is the true path to a satisfying existence. Perhaps this feline god can serve as inspiration for this idea, too.

MAFDET

Often drawn with the body of a woman and the head of a cheetah or lioness, Mafdet was most often portrayed with a desert lynx's head, sometimes with a crown of slithering serpents, and a thick tail. She is one of the earliest recorded Egyptian feline goddesses from the Old Kingdom of the First Dynasty, possibly even slightly predating Bastet and Sekhmet.

Mafdet was a savage goddess and a guardian of Osiris, a supreme god and mythological ruler of Egypt. She was also one of Ra's allies when he fought the reptilian demons of the Underworld. This led to one of Mafdet's titles, Slayer of Serpents, and people called upon her to protect them against poisonous snakes and scorpions.

Like all cat gods, Mafdet had several cults in her honor. One of the funeral rituals embraced by her followers was to place a coffin or corpse upon a cart that resembled a large cat. It had a carved cat head at the front and a tail fabricated of cloth or feathers flowing behind it. This prestigious carriage would transport the body with appropriate reverence to the burial site where the departing soul could be released back into the universal Divine Feline Energy from whence the world began, according to cat god worshippers.

Mafdet was considered a crusader for justice, a judge, and a punisher of crimes both on Earth and in the afterlife. As such, her devotees aimed to follow a good path in life, honoring both themselves and others. Mafdet was as dangerous as a venomous viper when protecting those she loved—an effective tool at keeping toxic people at bay. Today, in our explorations of inner well-being and self-care, we could also call upon Mafdet to help us fight our own worst enemies, such as self-doubt and insecurity.

MNGWA

This mythical cat, also called Nunda in Swahili, originates in Tanzania. The name translates to something along the lines of "strange one." According to a native song, this demonic feline figure is said to be stronger than a lion and more cunning than a leopard. He is described as resembling a gigantic tabby cat with gray and black tigerlike stripes and a long tail. Moving swiftly and silently, he could snatch a human in an instant, with the victim's mauled body often found clutching tufts of fluffy gray fur—a sure sign that Mngwa was to blame, which created public panic.

One folktale says that this beast originated as a small, striped kitten who was a sultan's pet. However, he eventually grew as large as a house and had such an insatiable appetite that he began to devour the townspeople's chickens, goats, oxen, and camels. Soon, children and fully grown adults went missing from surrounding villages. When word of Mngwa spread, the people believed that the merciless magical cat could catch anyone by surprise at any moment and hunt him down. Meanwhile, the sultan defended his cat and forbade anyone to harm him until the day arrived when Mngwa mercilessly killed three of the sultan's own six sons. At that point, the youngest son, who had barely escaped with his life, took down the giant kitty demon.

Be it the influence of tall tales or a remaining fear of this giant fluffy-tailed cat, people claimed to see a Mngwa roaming in the woods as late as the twentieth century. Is it possible that the phantom of this mystical feline continues to roam the forest? Or perhaps these are descendants of the overgrown tabby who was some kind of elusive wildcat. As late as the 1920s, parties were sent out to track down this vicious ghoul, but nobody ever succeeded in killing or capturing one.

To this day, the story of the Mngwa remains a curious tale the likes of Sasquatch or the Loch Ness Monster. Could it be that, like other mythological characters, he was simply a larger-than-life feline freak of nature with an outsize appetite rather than an evil being from the Underworld? Maybe the sultan was right to defend his pet friend as a misunderstood and misguided misfit, and if he were guided rather than feared, there could have been a different outcome for all. Perhaps the lesson from the sad and bloody legacy of the Mngwa is to see a troublesome situation from many different perspectives rather than jump to accusations. Or, it could simply be to pay close attention if your cuddly kitten seems to be growing larger than your entire abode.

MUEZZA

In Islamic tradition, cats are generally well thought of, and in various scriptures, the prophet Muhammad is said to have exalted them. Like Buddha and Jesus, Muhammad lived as a shining example of compassion toward all sentient beings, an example that is not always followed. Stories of animal sacrifice appear in the Bible, Koran, and Torah. Did the leaders of these religions really want people to hurt animals in their honor? Modern priests even declare that humans are the only animals to have souls, which does not make sense if an almighty god created all the living creatures.

Over the centuries, it has been convenient for humans to accept that their lives are worth more than those of animals. Due to this, most of the other species on our planet have been subject to poor treatment, even abuse. Factory farming, hunting endangered species such as lions and tigers for sport, horse racing, bullfighting, overbreeding expensive cats and dogs for profit—all these activities are justified because our modern world does not encourage respect for animals, and even more so because gods in their likenesses have faded away. The story of Muezza is one that pleases animal lovers because it shows extraordinary thoughtfulness toward this beloved cat.

Legend says that one morning the prophet Muhammad was preparing himself to attend morning prayer. When he went to dress, he found Muezza happily snoozing on the arm of his robe. Looking upon the cat resting there so peacefully filled his heart with love. (Hasn't every cat lover fawned over an adorable sleeping kitten?) Not wanting to disturb Muezza, Muhammad ever so gently cut the sleeve off his garment and softly pet the slumbering fur baby three times before leaving.

His loving act of kindness blessed all cats with the ability to land squarely on their feet and attract angels into the home where they live. In modern-day cities in Turkey, for example, many feral cat colonies are seen as communal pets and people are banned from harming them. This lovely tradition dates to the fourteenth century during the rule of the Ottoman Empire.

Did Muezza really exist or was this cat a tool in a metaphor to encourage kindness? We cannot know for sure. However, Muezza's legend and legacy earn this feline a place among the cat deities. Being kind works like magic. By improving the life of someone else, or at least showing them a thoughtful deed, we create an upward spiral that raises positive energy for everyone, even ourselves.

MUT

The Egyptian word *mut* means "mother," so it is not surprising that this deity is a primal mother goddess, sometimes portrayed as a grandmother, even outranking Isis. Some stories say that Mut gave birth to the world, so she is often drawn holding an *ankh*, or Egyptian key of life, which is an oval shape with a cross beneath it. Although she sometimes appears with a vulture's head, Mut is more commonly seen with the head of a lioness.

She was part of one of several triads of ancient Thebes. In one version, Mut was the wife or consort of Ra, and their son was Khonsu, god of the moon. There are a lot of crossovers between the many wives of Ra, and of course, there is overlap between various lion goddesses. However, one of Mut's defining attributes is her double crown combining the red of upper Egypt and white of lower Egypt, demonstrating that she was one of the more widely recognized goddesses.

Mut's maternal energy lends her a gentleness, and she may softly drop messages into the dreams of her devotees. Many people seek guidance from their subconscious, which is the basis of most modern psychoanalysis. Journaling is an effective way to connect with the wisdom residing just beyond our waking mind. Writing down thoughts and images that come to us during our slumbering hours are amazingly potent when working through problems or emotional challenges.

NERGAL

This destructive Mesopotamian god was worshipped for many centuries despite his reputation for killing repeatedly and without remorse. He was described as a furious lion and sometimes a raging bull, because he rampaged and destroyed whole cities when angered. We should, perhaps, refer to him more as a demon than a deity because he was a god of Kur, the Mesopotamian Underworld primarily associated with murder, death, and disease.

Some believe that his presence in the leonine pantheon was to serve as a kind of scapegoat for human suffering. When fires destroyed homes, children were taken by disease, and crops were overrun with pests, it was easier to shake proverbial fists at Nergal than feel helpless in the face of natural disasters. Much like our own pet cats, it was said that when Nergal was bored and needed to burn off excess energy, he enjoyed randomly knocking things over, such as buildings, and generally creating havoc in the way a violent sandstorm might pummel its way across the landscape.

His extensive cult spanned throughout Babylonia from modern-day Iraq to Greece. He remained prominent in the mythology in Assyria in later years and was regarded as one of the most important gods. Due to his fearful nature, Nergal was often depicted holding a mace with three lion-shaped heads, a dagger, and a bow.

When considering the primal power of Nergal and the ways a faithful feline god worshipper might harness some of it, take a moment to consider the consequences of dramatic actions. Turning fury upon another person may not deliver the desired outcome. However, summoning one's courage to confront an adversary, at work or in a personal relationship, is sometimes exactly what is needed to resolve a conflict. This is a positive approach to calling upon Nergal's aid in mustering the spiritual strength to take action.

QADESH

· · · · · · · · ·

This Semitic goddess was referred to as the Lion Lady. Her name has also been written as Kadesh, Qetesh, and Qudshu in some texts, and it is possible that Qadesh is an interpretation of the earlier Canaanite goddess called Asherah who was one of three main deities in their pantheon. Qadesh became incorporated into the Egyptian lion goddesses during the New Kingdom, and similar to other lion deities, she represented the cycles of nature, beauty, sexuality, and fertility. She was said to be like a big cat herself, powerful and free, mating with whomever she desired.

She was often depicted naked, standing atop a divine lion, sometimes wearing a sun disc on her head and holding a snake in one hand and a lotus flower in the other. Qadesh was a holy woman, and like many priestesses of the time, she used sex as a tool in sacred rituals. For this reason, she was referred to as a prostitute in some texts when female sexual power was seen as a threat to the emerging patriarchal societies.

Animals have no judgment or condemnation around mating, so the idea of sex being a clandestine activity is a purely human construct. Certainly, "free love" can be problematic in the example of a man who wants certainty that a child born to his mate is his own offspring while a male lion will accept all the offspring in his pride as his own.

Looking through a spiritual lens, much punishment has been brought upon women who were deemed promiscuous according to religious rules of behavior. The sexual liberation movement of the 1960s was a kind of psychic awakening that being godlike has nothing to do with being chaste. Rather than judging others, we can focus instead on our own spiritual growth, in whatever form that might take, including sexual exploration. This would be walking the path of Qadesh, who fits the description of a modern feminist goddess who is still relevant in our time.

SEKHMET

Depicted with a strong, beautiful womanly body clothed in red robes and a lion's head, Sekhmet is Bastet's sister. It is said that she was born from the fire in Ra's eye, and atop her flowing mane she wore a sun disc encircled by the uraeus serpent, or upright cobra. Sekhmet carries a papyrus scepter and the ankh sign (a teardrop-shaped hoop with a cross below it) in her hands, which represents her capacity to give life and fertility through the yearly Nile floods in Egypt. Along with her sister, Bastet, she too was a consort of Ptah, and their son was Nefertem, who is often shown with a blue lotus flower as a sort of crown and sometimes with the head of a lion. This family of three was also referred to as the Memphite triad.

Because Bastet and Sekhmet have both been depicted with a lion's head and are known to have a wild streak, and they both have offspring with Ptah, they are sometimes confused for each other in ancient lore. Even their children get ascribed to the wrong mother. However, one clear distinction is that their followers were divided geographically as Sekhmet was the deity of upper Egypt, while Bastet oversaw the lower part of the country.

Her name comes from the Egyptian word *sekhem*, which translates to "powerful." Like her famed sibling, Sekhmet had a dangerous duality, in her case as both a fiery destructor and a benevolent healer. She could be blamed for bringing a plague down upon a community in one instance and then be called upon to cure the disease in another. In her role as a mighty war goddess, she aided pharaohs in battle by breathing hot air across the desert, blinding their enemies with the hot air that burned their eyes in a sandstorm. Banners bearing her name and likeness were often paraded into battle in an attempt to intimidate enemies and summon the goddess's aid.

Sekhmet seems to have originated in the Delta area, where there were few wild lions. Therefore, the beasts were considered magical, which gave the lion-headed goddess even more mystique. Her cult followers were centered in Luxor,

Memphis, and Letopolis, and they were a bloodthirsty lot, killing animals as offerings to her. In Greece, the city of the lion, or Leontopolis, had many of her followers, and tamed lions and lionesses were kept in the temples to serve as living totems in her honor. Priests in her following were so terrified of displeasing Sekhmet that they performed rituals before statues of her every day.

Hundreds of larger-than-life statues of Sekhmet have been unearthed, a testament to her importance. They are displayed at museums and historical sites around the world, and the fine details reveal feline expressions, radiant hair, and elegant jewelry. What is most interesting, perhaps, is the desecration of these statues over various time periods. Some of the effigies were viciously attacked, and hands and feet cut off. This may have been an attempt by some who feared the goddess and tried to render her magic impotent.

Sekhmet had a thirst for destruction, and as she was finding footing in her visits to this earthly plane at times went on killing sprees and gorged herself on the blood of the pitiful human race. When her father, Ra, recognized that this wildcat was out of control, he ordered the people to mix pomegranate juice with strong beer to trick her into thinking she was drinking blood. However, she greedily lapped up so much of it that she passed out for three days from what amounted to alcohol poisoning. When she recovered, her bloodlust had subsided.

On the sunnier side of this terrifying deity, Sekhmet was referred to as the Mistress of Life and was associated with healing and medicine. She was the patron of healers, and the priests in her temples were skilled physicians who served as mediums for her messages and miracles. The faithful also whispered prayers into the ears of mummified cats offered to her in attempts to win her favor.

With the new year, the people danced, sang, played music, got inebriated, and rutted like the beasts they were, smeared with pomegranate juice, wine, and beer. This crazy ritual was also a sort of "anti–rain dance" to prevent the Nile from over-flooding as too much runoff encouraged mosquitoes and disease. This part of the great river ran bloodred when it swept clay silt upstream. Today, devotees still drink beer colored with red pomegranate juice at celebrations in Sekhmet's honor, though orgies are no longer an official event.

People who incorporate Sekhmet into modern spiritual practices would be wise to consider using their inner fire to protect those they love. Earning the respect of our communities doesn't come through forcing our will onto others but rather by leading by example. Donating money or volunteering hours to a cat rescue would please the feline goddess. Fostering motherless kittens, walking dogs who are suffering from lack of exercise at animal shelters, or donating to wild animal protection organizations are ways to bring the positive aspects of these deities into the world today.

TEFNUT

· · · · · · · · · ·

This Egyptian goddess of rain and her twin brother, Shu, God of Wind, are yet more members of the lion-headed family of deities. Their father was the sun god Ra who sired many gods, quite a few of whom have feline qualities. Hathor is credited with being the twins' mother. Tefnut is said to have mated with her brother and they produced two children—Nut, God of the Sky, and Geb, Guardian of the Earth.

Tefnut's nickname was She Who Spits, which could be attributed to her association with falling raindrops. By being associated with water, which is the symbol of life in the desert, she was the lion goddess most closely linked with survival. People lifted their voices to her in hopes she would sprinkle water upon the farmlands.

By many accounts, though, she was also another fickle goddess. When droughts and wars came, she was credited with turning the tears of sorrow into the seeds of vengeance. At other times, she took the form of a fierce lioness who could embody the burning sun itself, which dried up the crops and starved the people who angered her. Upon their demise, legends recounted that she would wet the land with their blood—quite a vivid image!

Perhaps the lesson we can take from Tefnut is not to take others for granted. Tefnut represented a source of life who supported humans' well-being when she was treated with reverence. She could also turn her back with cold cruelty if she was not happy. If we think about our own fickle feline fur babies, their "turn on a dime" personalities are not so different from this temperamental goddess.

AMERICAS

he Indigenous people of North, Central, and South America developed a spiritual relationship with the land and with nature. It is impossible to generalize when covering the incredibly diverse terrains, climates, and civilizations that have inhabited these continents, but they share a connection to animals as guides and fellow citizens of earth in their religions. This appreciation has been passed down through generations of storytelling, pottery, dances, and songs, and it is even represented by the very early dwellers through ancient drawings on cave walls. In one form or another, many of these spiritual practices continue today.

At native festivals and feast-day celebrations, traditional dancers still dress in costumes adorned with feathers, shells, horsehair, animal skins, teeth, and claws. The movements, set to drumbeats and rhythmic bells or chanting, mimic the soaring eagle, the thundering buffalo, the graceful deer, and a myriad of other animals. One Navajo belief is that if a shaman travels by night, he should wear the skin of a predatory animal for protection. Many animal hides are used in Native American traditions, and the mountain lion skin is one that was used for this purpose as the cats have keen eyes in the dark and could easily camouflage themselves against the mountains.

The wily coyote makes appearances in traditional tales as do snakes, weasels, and bears. At times they are friends, and at other times they are foes, but each has its place in a labyrinth of narratives from creation through the end of the world. While the populations dotting the vast expanse from the northern reaches of Canada to the southern tip of Argentina varied tremendously, we have overwhelming evidence that wildcats held a deep and meaningful place in native worship.

Despite differing markings, sizes, colors, and habitats, the admirable qualities these fantastical felines displayed stay relatively consistent—grace, stealth, and wisdom. There is great diversity within the cats of the Americas, and even as conservationists are fighting to save their dwindling populations, many still roam modern-day forests and jungles. In North America, the puma, also referred to as a cougar or mountain lion, is considered the most fearless of animal guides by Hopi and neighboring tribes, and a central figure in many holy ceremonies despite also being killed for its hide.

The North American lynx has had several roles in Native American folklore. It is respected for its hunting skills yet, at times, portrayed as foolishly outwitted by lesser animals and humans. Other communities, such as those among the Anishinaabe tribes of the Great Lakes region, consider the lynx to be a spirit animal of the Midewiwin medicine men.

From southern Mexico through Central America and some parts of South America, the tiny, nocturnal margay with its round eyes and velvety, patterned coat lives in dark recesses of the green forests. Their population has also been at risk because their cuddly house cat appearance makes them appealing exotic pets on the black market despite their somewhat ferocious nature. Associated with loyalty, intelligence, and stealth, the spiritual impact of this cat not only touches those regions but is also depicted on ritualistic objects as far away as Japan and China.

Ocelots span a similar region as margay. These endangered cats hide in deep brush, mangroves, and tropical forests. Considered shamanic messengers, they deliver solutions to troubling situations through dreams and the tingling sensation of deep intuition.

Of all the wildcats in the Americas, however, none is as revered as the majestic jaguar. Not only is it physically the largest feline in the Americas, but it also carries enormous cultural impact across the eighteen countries where it lives. Jaguars can be all black or golden with black spots, like a cheetah, with the difference being that jaguars have black rosettes in the middle of their dark blotches.

Unlike many other big cats, jaguars hunt both day and night and they are one of the few who swim. The presence of jaguars reflects the health of a region's biodiversity because they help regulate the populations of smaller species. After being hunted to extinction in the United States, conservationists are now working on the Jaguar Corridor Initiative with local governments and community groups to help the cats occupy wild spaces from Mexico to Argentina.

In Mayan and Mexican cultures, the jaguar is known as Balam and represents the life force pulsing through nature, in this case, Divine Feline Energy. It can also mean "priest" or "sorcerer." From fertile crops to political maneuvering, community leaders looked to the spirit of the jaguar for guidance. However, the fickle nature of cats led people to vacillate between worship and distrust of their feline deities. The Aztecs also built temples to honor the jaguar gods, and jaguars themselves were believed to have the ability to cross between worlds. Jaguar gods are associated with all aspects of life, and some believed that holy people could transform into jaguars requiring human sacrifices as offerings.

Just as the Greeks and Romans had families of gods and goddesses, the people of Mesoamerica had their own pantheon of gods based on the majestic jaguar. While jaguars appear in most of the ancient cultures from this area, they are predominantly Mayan, and they have at least eight jaguar gods. In some historical accounts, there is even mention of a jaguar house in the Underworld. Some of the gods were associated with lucky numbers, such as four and seven. There are also the Hero Twin jaguars, named Hun-ahpu and Xbalanque, who balanced each other in their opposition. One was mild mannered and the other violent. There is also the Jaguar Baby, who may have been associated with blood sacrifice, and the Water Lily Jaguar.

Jaguars lived in close proximity to the people, and the mighty cats were respected for their brute strength and cunning strategy when hunting. The pattern of their coats was likened to the stars dotted across the night sky. It also served as useful camouflage, making them elusive when being hunted or stalking prey. These physical qualities were considered magical and attributed to a higher power. Some Mayan rulers incorporated the word for jaguar into their own names when they took power and had jaguar images on their clothing. Thrones often had jaguars painted upon them and carved into them, and some were even fashioned to resemble the body of a jaguar.

To this day, La Danza de Los Tecuanes, or the Dance of the Jaguars, is performed at festivals. This is an interpretive reenactment of two warring tribes that conspire to capture the jaguar who had been terrorizing local villages. Participating in this dance honoring the beautiful but deadly wildcat is said to bring forth powerful human emotions ranging from violence to benevolence, drawing from the jaguar gods' shamanic energy.

The Aztecs similarly held the jaguar in high regard and considered it to be the spiritual representation of their primary deity, Tezcatlipoca. He was a shape-shifting ruler of the night, warrior, and overseer of the Earth who could be both ferociously destructive and a great protector. When he took the form of a jaguar, he was called Tepeyollotl.

Today, we find spiritual remnants of the holy jaguar in every country of the Americas. In Colombia, the Arhuaco consider the jaguar to be a wise sage. The Bororó in Bolivia and Brazil regard the jaguar as the bearer of spiritual strength. The Matsés people living along the Peruvian border with Bolivia call on the jaguar to connect with their own inner warrior when they need bolstering in times of crisis, going as far as donning fangs and tattooing catlike characteristics on their faces such as whiskers and jaguar spots.

In Peru, the Chavín culture was built on a foundation of nature spirits including an all-powerful feline god. The belief in a cat deity spread through the eastern jungles, coastal valleys, and mountainous villages of the Andes. The Chavín cult, as it was later known, was responsible for the construction of many temples in treacherous corners of wild spaces where the nature gods could be suitably worshipped. They were also gifted with talents in stone carving and metallurgy, making use of the silver, gold, and copper mined from the mountains.

Some Indigenous communities still invoke the power of the jaguar through their shamans when partaking in mind-altering ayahuasca ceremonies. During these events, inner wisdom, emotions, and dreams reveal themselves, and some say that the jaguar spirit takes over the body. Needless to say, jaguars remain highly respected among the Amazonian tribes who live a more reclusive, ancient lifestyle.

AGASSOU

This Haitian cat god originates in Dahomey, an ancient kingdom in West Africa located in modern-day Benin. His story was brought to the Caribbean by the people who were kidnapped or sold into slavery and transported over the ocean. Like many deities and spiritual practices that originated in parts of Africa and are still practiced today in the United States and Caribbean islands, Agassou is related to voodoo practices. Because of the connection with boats, he is a water deity and is said to have the power to turn people's hands into stiff catlike claws when angered.

Agassou is the magical offspring of a feline god who mated with a human. He is sometimes called the Leopard Spirit and could shape-shift into either a leopard or a person, whichever best served him in the moment. He was a kingly god, and the Dahomeyan royal family chose Agassou as its patron and the leopard as its animal totem.

Are there parts of your life that have become rigid like a finger turned into a stiff cat claw? Where can you create more movement and spiritual flow? Like a leopard who can easily seek camouflage due to its rosette spots, having the flexibility to explore the world around you without risk of judgment—from yourself or others—can provide the path to inner freedom.

AI APAEC

This bloodthirsty demon was associated with magical wild-cats. Depicted as a decrepit old man with tigerlike fangs and long kitty whiskers, Ai Apaec hails from the pre-Inca Mochica people in the mountainous area of modern-day Peru. He wore a belt made of venomous serpents and a crown with a jaguar's head as its centerpiece, all of which connected him with both the sun gods and the masters of the Underworld. His magical powers allowed him to pass through the veils between worlds.

Ai Apaec was known as a cruel deity who demanded the sacrifice of strong, young warriors in exchange for victory in warfare. These horrific rituals happened at temples of the moon and the temple of the witches, among others. Despite this gruesome appetite, he was considered to be the god of creation and a protector of the Moche world.

What do we think of the warriors who were sacrificed to please a glorious god? Are they to be pitied for being murdered in the prime of their lives, or did they go proudly and honorably to a death fit for a respected martyr? What do we sacrifice for victory in our own lives? Is the time we exchange for money worth the investment? Do we give too much to an unsatisfactory relationship? Achieving our greatness means constantly evaluating what we expend for the reward we get. Keeping those things in balance keeps life moving in the desired direction.

BALAM NAHN

· · · · · · · · ·

The Water Lily Jaguar was a major deity associated with royalty because elite members of society wore lilies in their hair when they had access to them. Water lilies also have spiritual connections in many religious traditions from historic Egypt—where they were considered to ward off evil spirits—to Christianity, where water lilies' interlocking petals symbolized the unity of all life. In Buddhism, the water lily is associated with rebirth. At one Mayan royal burial ground at Tikal in Guatemala, a three-pound jade water lily jaguar statue was unearthed, demonstrating the significance of both jaguar gods and the sacred flower.

We can tell this jaguar god is differentiated from the others because she is adorned with water lily flowers or petals upon her head, and sometimes the lilies serve as a necklace. In other cases, the feline form in a carving or painting is completely covered with blossoms. In the latter depiction, the Water Lily Jaguar can be a deity of love, likened to the Roman Venus or the Greek Aphrodite.

The Water Lily Jaguar goddess was also associated with celebrations and libations, the kind that might be imbibed in ceremonies or poured out as a sacrifice. In this way, this spirit could also be likened to Libertas or Bacchus from the Romans or Artemis or Dionysus from the Greeks. Because these flowers bloomed in the rainy season, Balam Nahn was considered a fertility deity as well.

Perhaps we can think of the Water Lily Jaguar as extending an invitation to live our best lives. That could include sharing a glass of bubbly with friends and toasting to our most cherished dreams and accomplishments. Or maybe it is simply beautifying our surroundings with fresh stems from the garden, farmers market, or corner store. Living royally does not require empires and temples in our honor but rather an appreciation for moments of indulgence.

CARBUNCLO

This mystical catlike creature is identified by haunting demonic eyes that glow red, like hot coals, and some stories say that his body emits a bluish-white light. This otherworldly quality illuminates his path as he crosses wooded areas at night or scurries along dark underground tunnels as he travels deep into mines.

Carbunclo hails from South American folklore, and as may be assumed from his description, he is popular in the mining community. His name comes from the Latin word *carbunculus* or "little coal." Despite his own creepy appearance, Carbunclo is afraid of humans. If he senses a person or any other kind of predator nearby, a shell-like hump on his back slaps shut, so the soft light emanating from within his thin skin cannot be detected. He can then sit very still and be mistaken for a rock.

Stories from Argentina, Chile, and Paraguay are rife with varying details about Carbunclo, and each is more bizarre than the next. For example, some say that the protective lid that hides his glowing skin is covered with beautiful, down-like feathers. Others denote his ability to move as quickly as lightning and leap swiftly up rocky trails, his whiskers and bearded chin aglow. Then there is the headpiece he sometimes dons, dotted with a mosaic of shiny slivers of reflective glass and sparkling rubies.

Obviously, with all this bling, Carbunclo is associated with jewels and precious metals. Anyone who catches sight of this mysterious shell-backed feline ghoul is about to receive abundant wealth. Miners and prospectors have set about hunting these magical creatures, hoping to steal his crown or find the stash of gold and gems he may have hidden in his own den. Alas, he has not been caught and the legend of the elusive nocturnal and bejeweled cat spirit lives on. Perhaps the real moral of the tale is to search for the true value below the surface in the people and experiences in your life. Not all that glitters is worth the literal or proverbial treasures of Carbunclo.

CCOA

From the mythology of the Quechua tribe in southern Peru comes the Ccoa—a large demonic cat spirit who is said to have dark stripes and lives between slivers of shadowed rocks in the Andes. The Apus are mountain deities who protected the people below, and this Ccoa was a sort of divine pet belonging to them. His fierce puma face was seen in the night sky, which included the evening star. Ancient people would peer upward with reverence for the shimmering spirit.

The Ccoa was associated with water, so during the wet season he was said to sneak down from the mountains with his long tail sweeping across the clouds, letting loose great torrents of rain and hail. He was also believed to be able to fly, and when doing so, he could urinate rain and shoot bolts of lightning from his eyes. His large figure was said to block the sun and moon during eclipses.

While most people die from lightning strikes, the sorcerers and witches caught in the Ccoa's electrical storms only became even more powerful. Because of this, he was seen as an accomplice in black magic. Practitioners of the spiritual dark arts made offerings to the Ccoa in gratitude for their special powers. They also buried the bodies of unbaptized babies in the mountains as offerings to him. Other gifts that pleased the Ccoa included incense, wine, silver, and gold, which are likely associated with the feline-worshipping Chavín cult.

The people we most associate with will determine the outcome of our lives. Fear and rage are fed with negative thoughts and actions. Naysayers, gossips, and untrustworthy or false friends dim our own creative light. We must let them go because they hold us back from achieving inner peace. Engaging with optimistic people who are solution seekers with kind intentions will protect our psyches from dark energy.

EK BALAM

Ek Balam was said to see into the darkness of the universe and impart wisdom to his followers. Through internal visions and outward signs, he was able to send messages. For example, a jaguar sighting was often considered an omen of conflict on the horizon, preparing the people to be vigilant. Like many jaguar gods, Ek Balam was respected for both his valor and ferocity, making him emblematic of facing an enemy or challenge with courage.

The famous Ek Balam ruins on Mexico's Yucatán Peninsula have been a source of fascination for historians for many years and were built in honor of their namesake god, which had the nicknames Black God or Bright Star Jaguar. The site has more than forty-five structures, which include two palaces, a large pyramid, and multiple temples. There is also a famous tower that houses a tomb of Ek Balam's ruler, Ukil-Kan-Lek-Tok. Rather than carvings, it was decorated with a limestone mortar molded into figures on the surface of the structure.

The Ek Balam site opened as a cultural attraction for researchers and visitors about a decade after being mapped in the 1980s. It is located near the colonial-era city of Valladolid and is a popular tourist attraction today for those hoping to get a glimpse into the Mayan way of life. It is northeast of the famed Chichén Itzá pyramids and was likely built about two thousand years ago. It was in use for about a millennium, and some historians determined that people could still have been living there when the Spanish invaded the area in the 1600s.

This jaguar god is a symbol of mustering strength and determination to face challenges and conflicts. When a situation feels heavy and it is not easy to see a way out, feline lovers can look for the light of their own intuition guided by Ek Balam. Calling upon the Bright Star Jaguar god or if you are looking for a sign, a black cat crossing your path can be taken as a good omen for your dilemma.

GOD L

· · · · · · · · · ·

God L is associated with sorcery and is one of the oldest Mayan jaguar deities. As an ancient god of the Underworld, he is also associated with skyward displays such as lightning, thunder, and torrential storms. He is the patron of merchants, and has the authoritative air of a strict father.

In many representations, God L is shown as a wise old man who guides mortals seeking the afterlife. He presides over many other gods and is said to be attended by other young gods in the Underworld. He is often pictured with catlike ears—those of a jaguar—and wears a headdress of owl feathers, a bird who is also associated with both wisdom and the dark world beyond. Sometimes, this aged deity appears surrounded by smoke and smoking a ceremonial pipe or cigars, hence his nickname the Smoking God.

Like some jaguars, he appears to be black. The Maya used ashes and soot as well as clay made from volcanic soil to draw him on stone walls and caves. Although most of this coloring has washed away over time, traces remain, giving us clues to the appearance of this important feline deity.

His most famous depiction is at the Temple of the Cross in Palenque, Mexico, an important Mayan remnant in the state of Chiapas. The temple itself represents a doorway to Xibalba, the world beyond mortality, and each of the three main structures is dedicated to a god. Many elaborate, large carved bowls were used as incense burners and have been excavated around the area. Similar to other religions, including incense burned in high holy day Catholic masses, smoke was believed to carry prayers to the heavens.

The representations of this god are full of symbolic imagery, which give us insights into the animals valued in Mayan culture. Perhaps one way we can continue to preserve the living history of the people descended from this fascinating civilization is to protect the land and the animals who they hold dear. The ripple effects of conservation are most poignant at a local level, but nature is interconnected around the planet. There are no borders for air, animals, jungle, and water. By conserving one ecosystem, we create positive consequences for all.

HOKDIDASHA

The Zuni, or A-Shiwi, include the mountain lion, the wild bobcat, and lynx spirits among their gods overseeing specific areas of life. The yellow cat god, Hokdidasha, was guardian of the north and associated with personal power, resourcefulness, intuition, and loyalty, and the wildcat is thought of as a younger spiritual brother of the mountain lion who represents clairvoyance and secrets. These majestic felines were considered among the sacred hunting animals.

To this day, the Zuni people make fetishes, or animal-shaped carvings, as spiritual items. These are made in the forms of various animals and crafted from turquoise, bone, stone, or other organic materials. These totems are used in ceremonies, and each one has great significance and purpose. They are often ascribed healing and protective powers benefiting the artist who makes them as well as the person to whom they are gifted. They can be used to assist hunters as well as generally guarding people against bad spirits.

Fetishes are kept in small clay pots encrusted with turquoise or in blessed leather pouches. To keep one's fetish content, it must be given offerings of ground cornmeal mixed with turquoise dust. The pieces themselves are considered mystical medicine because the carvings can contain, or help connect with, sacred animal spirits.

Embodying the spirit of a fetish means staying true to your own spirit and listening for the healing wisdom that lives within each of us. When we are led astray by greed or insecurities, we are not honoring the people who came before us, the earth upon which we walk, or the Divine Feline Energy that flows through the wild cats and every being in the universe. Adding a mountain lion or bobcat fetish to your meditation altar can be a powerful tool in connecting with your own intuition and clairvoyance.

IX CHEL

Ix Chel is a Mayan deity and mother of gods. As with many ancient goddesses, there are several conflicting stories about Ix Chel. Her name is sometimes spelled Ixchel, Ixchebelyax, Ix Hunic, and Ix Huinieta, and she has been used interchangeably with other goddesses in some stories. She had the nickname Lady Rainbow and was sometimes called Goddess of the Moon. She is included in the pantheon of jaguar gods, and in various stories she is married to the Lord Jaguar of Terrestrial

Fire, while others say she was the wife of jaguar God L. Of her thirteen children, two were the powerful creators of heaven and Earth and all the beings who live within them.

Like many feline deities, she is associated with childbirth and fertility. Ix Chel was also said to have the ability to control cycles of the moon, which are, of course, similar to women's menstruating cycles. Her Aztec equivalent was Toci Yoalticitl, who was associated with sweat baths, popular places for giving birth in Aztec culture.

As the patron of midwifery, Ix Chel's female followers seeking a fruitful coupling would go to her temple on the island of Isla Mujeres, not far from Cancún, off the Yucatán Peninsula. There, the women would pray to be blessed with love and children. Some legends say that villages offered young unmarried women as blood sacrifices to her to ensure more babies born into their communities, while other accounts say that no killings should occur in her name.

Ix Chel was pleased by crafts such as textiles, and she was also called upon for her cunning guidance in the art of war. In some early accounts, she was shown with catlike claws on her feet and a snake around her neck. When angered, she could create storms and floods, which would certainly not be welcome on the little island where the remnants of her holy fertility sanctuary still exist today.

People often prayed to this goddess in hopes of fruitful unions especially when they wanted a baby. However, we can perceive being blessed with new life as taking many forms. For example, this could apply to a new creative project or a new way to think about a troubled relationship. Perhaps it would mean finding an answer to a problem long unsolved. Ix Chel is a goddess of implementing stability and finding a steady rhythm in times of chaos, and this is certainly helpful to all people navigating our turbulent modern world.

LUSIFEE

The name Lusifee was likely derived from the French-Canadian word for "lynx" or "loup-cervier," a sneaky and dangerous predator. Many early fur traders came from France, which influenced the language and lore as they carried their interpretation of native tales they heard along their journeys.

As a mystical cat, Lusifee has both positive and negative interpretations. Indigenous Canadian Wabanaki folklore recounts him as malevolent and greedy. However, the Zuni people in the United States revered the lynx wildcat spirit as a clairvoyant and helpful when searching for game.

He is included in various native legends, including one where he pursues a rabbit for his dinner. The rabbit is a trickster and dupes the hungry lynx several times. Finally, as revenge for trying to kill the rabbit, Lusifee has his eyes pecked out by ravens and is left for dead in the forest. Considering the circle of life in the wild—the hunters and their prey—this hardly seems fair, but it appears that the rabbit had the upper hand, after all. Because of this ordeal, some say that Lusifee's magical spirit still roams the woods and will assist human rabbit hunters as part of his own eternal vendetta.

The tale of this wildcat can be seen from several points of view. Whether siding with the hungry lynx or cheering for the clever bunny, perspective determines who is the hero and who is the villain. As with everything in life, attempting to view a situation from all sides leads to the most balanced evaluation of what is actually the truth.

MISHIPESHU

In the Great Lakes region of the United States, Indigenous people spoke of a powerful demon living in the dark recesses of deep water. It was described as a large-cat-meets-dragon with massive copper horns growing from its head symbolizing its divinity. Its body and long tail are covered in slippery copper scales.

Mishipeshu is often referred to as the Great Lynx with webbed feet, making it a swift swimmer. This powerful god was feared by the people living around the lakes because it would stir up waves, rapids, and whirlpools. The tumult it caused could even break the ice in winter, which caused people to fall in and drown. Children still sometimes play a game called Mishipeshu whereby they take turns embodying the monster and throwing one another into water.

As signaled by the copper elements on its body, the monster was the guardian of precious metals. As such, divers would brave the deep water hoping to find its stash of treasure. The Algonquin people believed that the horned snakes, and in particular the Great Lynx, were protective gods who could provide sustenance for the community. They also called upon Mishipeshu for assistance when fishing because its underwater movements could push fish to the surface of the water.

We could see the stirring of the underwater tides as a symbol of bringing inner troubles to the surface, which is the first step in healing old wounds. The Great Lynx might be a symbol for therapy, writing, purging long-held resentment, or otherwise facing personal pain and working through it. Once an issue is brought to light, it can be dealt with and let go.

TEPEYOLLOTL

Known as the Heart of the Mountain, this god is the protector of jaguars and big cats who roam the forests of North and Central America. In his humanlike form, he is called Tezcatlipoca and was worshipped by the Aztec, Tlaxcaltec, and Toltec peoples of Mesoamerica. His roots stretch back to the Mayan and Olmec civilizations, and like so many other gods, it is possible that the Aztecs created him as a new incarnation of a previously existing god. After all, the mighty jaguar figured prominently in all populations throughout these regions over many centuries.

Tepeyollotl is associated with obsidian, and the shamans who practiced rituals in his name would carry a piece of it or wear a carving—often of a jaguar—somewhere on their bodies while chanting or performing other spiritual acts. Obsidian was used to make mirrors at the time, which were also seen as somewhat magical or holy instruments as well as used for everyday grooming and preening by those privileged enough to own one.

As one of the central jaguar deities, Tepeyollotl was a shape-shifting ruler of the night overseeing mighty warriors. He could be both ferociously destructive to the Earth's inhabitants through natural disasters while also being called upon as a great protector. When displeased, it was believed that his thunderous roar took on a physical aspect as an earthquake. His voice echoed and reverberated through mountains and caves, and his spirit still resides in the dark spaces throughout the Earth. When he takes jaguar form, his many spots represent the stars in a dark night sky.

We all have the capacity to stay stuck in a painful dead end or to look for solutions. When navigating the feelings around a loss, we can dwell on what is not working for us or we can see if there might be a silver lining in a tough situation—a way through the darkness that we had not yet considered. Try calling upon the Heart of the Mountain for the protection of your heart as a resolution comes to pass.

ASIA

. . . .

When thinking of mythological beings in Asian cultures, certainly dragons are the first to come to mind. Indeed, since 5000 BCE, dragons symbolize power, strength, and good luck and are considered insightful and caring allies to human beings. However, big cats rival their place within the myriad of godlike animals or animallike gods.

Of course, it is impossible to generalize the spirituality of Asia as a whole. The large geographical area is comprised of many countries, languages, traditions, and varying religions and folklore. Still, like Africa, the Americas, and Europe, there are some common threads and themes that run through shared mystical beliefs.

For example, the tiger represents aggressive qualities such as strength by force but is also a symbol of honor. Some wild tigers are found roaming remote pockets of China and India, although their populations are rapidly dwindling there as well as in other Asian countries due to habitat loss and illegal hunting. The high mountains of Bhutan and Nepal have seen slight increases in tiger births and even occasional sightings of snow leopards because of conservation efforts, though much more needs to be done to save these regal creatures from disappearing forever.

Two epic tales from ancient Indian literature feature cats as prominent characters. Around 400 BCE, the Mahabharata includes the cat Lomasa who befriends a mouse named Palita. Rather than eat the little rodent, they have lengthy discussions about relationships and other philosophical topics. In the Ramayana, the god Indra transforms himself into a cat to sneak out of his lover's home before her husband returns. Even the story of *Puss in Boots* popularized by the French author Charles Perrault in the late seventeenth century has roots in Indian literature.

Lions are also important deity spirits. Sometimes the mythological figures are lionlike, and some are combinations of animals. China has an abundance of such creatures. Pixiu has the head of a dragon atop a lion's body. It flies through the sky, protecting the gates of heaven. The Zheng is a leopard with five tails and a horn growing out of its head with a howl as loud as thunder. A taotie has a goat's body, human head and hands, and tiger's teeth. This one is sent to Earth to devour gluttonous people. The Zhu Jian has a cyclops head—human in form with one large eye—and the body of a leopard, horns, and a long tail. Yet another tale says that the qilin appeared at the birth of Confucius bearing a book made of jade. The book proclaimed the baby as the reincarnation of the God of Water, a symbol associated with the ancient teacher. The qilin was said to have the body of an elk and the head of a lion set with tiger eyes.

In one Chinese story about the creation of the world, cats were so valued that they were given the ability to speak and help oversee the other beings. However, the cats were easily distracted and enjoyed dozing in shady spots beneath the trees.

When the gods continually found these master kitties sleeping on the job, they finally took away their power of speech and gave it to the humans instead. Given the troubles in our modern world, we could wonder if this was the best decision after all.

People who observe the Lunar New Year, which follows the Chinese Zodiac calendar, may have noticed there is not a year of the cat, which seems a bit odd considering that tigers and lions are vital symbols. There is yet another interesting story to explain why this is so. Legend says that the cat and rat were close friends but that the rat betrayed the cat and took his spot in the zodiac lineup on the day that animals were being assigned their place.

Cats were brought to Japan around AD 500 by ships that docked on the islands. After serving their time on the floating vessels, the kitties disembarked, found their own little corners to start a new life, and began to procreate. Like humans around the globe had done for centuries, the local people found them useful as pest control around food storage areas. However, the monks in Buddhist temples found that the cats had an even higher calling. Rodents often found their way to parchment scrolls, chewing their way through sacred ancient texts. Cats became protectors of this scripture as well as beloved companions to the solitary inhabitants of these hallowed places.

Perhaps this favorable view of cats among the holy people is what led to the concept of cats being lucky in Japanese culture. There are many tales of cats bringing good fortune to humans. One such story involves a nobleman walking along a road when a cat, near a temple across the way, beckoned to him by raising one paw. The man crossed the road to investigate, and a bolt of lightning struck where the man had previously been walking.

By saving the man's life, the cat was considered a good omen—a "lucky cat." Also referred to as Maneki Neko, this kind of *yōkai* is a shape-shifting creature from ancient Japanese folklore and mythology. The lucky cat statuettes continue to be part of pop culture today and are commonly found in Asian businesses and homes.

However, it must be acknowledged that in Japan, as well as other Asian countries, mystical cats have also been portrayed as demons, bringing bad fortune. For example, the Bakeneko and Nekomata are demon cats who would eat humans in order to take on their form. The Kinkwa Neko, also called Golden Flower Cat, could disguise herself as a beautiful woman who would also snack on the flesh of humans who dared to come near her. In Thailand, the Phi Cha Kla is a dark-colored cat

demon whose fur grows back to front. He hides from humans, but if a person happens to find him and peer into his ghostly, hypnotic red eyes, they will soon die. Encountering both benevolent and malevolent cat spirits merely represents the duality of all human life—dark and light, good and bad, yin and yang exist in the nature of all beings.

Geographically, Turkey sits partly in Europe and partly in Asia and is a longtime cat-loving country. There are many cats strolling the streets, which can be alarming to visitors who don't realize that people in the towns often adopt these cat colonies. These cat lovers bring food and keep an eye on the kitties living semi-ferally. Of course, for anyone tending to a cat colony, capturing the cats to get them spayed and neutered is integral to controlling their populations and well-being. Often, once the cat is neutered, it is returned to its colony. This can be coordinated with a local animal shelter in most places. A popular saying in ancient Arabic states that if someone kills a cat, they should build a mosque to be forgiven. Perhaps creating a new cat rescue group would be an even better idea.

A love for felines continues to this day. In 2023, a Turkish author named Sunay Akin founded Cat Museum Istanbul with a goal to further passion for environmental conservation and preservation in young people. The museum features cat figurines, artwork, and stories regaling these beloved animals, which he believes are most connected to humans throughout civilizations.

Some of the cat gods and demons in this section are rather obscure, making research particularly challenging with regard to name spellings. It is possible that a cat deity is known by more than one name and appears in multiple cultures with slight variations.

BAGHESHUR

Wild tigers in India are reflected in spiritual practices, and Lord Shiva himself is known as a tiger god. Bagheshur is one such striped feline god who has been revered by the citizens in central India for thousands of years. The Baiga people, in particular, are an ancient tribe who hold him in high regard and consider themselves descendants of the tiger god.

This deity is said to bring rain when pleased and drought when insulted, resulting in poor crops. He also protects people from wild tiger attacks in jungle areas if they leave him bowls of gruel as offerings. Bonobibi, a goddess who is considered the Queen of the Forest, is appreciated by both Hindus and Muslims. She rides a sacred tiger, such as Bagheshur, through the wilds to protect people when they go into jungles and woods to gather firewood or fish.

All societies believe they are descended from gods in some way. Christians believe they are made in the likeness of God while others connect with animal deities. What this concept really drives home is the need to protect nature, which supports all life. Water, air, plants, and animals are integral to human life and therefore sacred no matter what form of spirituality someone follows.

BAKENEKO

This Japanese *yōkai* appears as a magical cat who can speak human languages and resurrect the dead. The Bakeneko were also said to grow long tails to help them walk and run upright and even dance. What a marvelous sight that would be! Sadly, this superstition led to the cruel practice of people cropping the tails of kittens to avoid them developing this fabled skill. It was also believed that the family cat could potentially become magical over time, and, if so, its powers would only strengthen as the years went on. Tragically, out of fear, older cats were sometimes discarded.

This heartless treatment of felines did not bode well for the family if their cat was, indeed, enchanted, because the Bakeneko were vengeful creatures. When the Bakeneko grew into its powerful midlife years, it was sometimes referred to as a Nekomata. If its tail was left intact, it would split in half, allowing it even more advanced upright movement. Left alone and angry, these dancing, cavorting creatures could cause chaos across whole villages.

Some courtesans were believed to be Nekomata in disguise, tempting men to hand over their fortunes, and in some cases, their lives. Through this, the Nekomata would become wealthy and, therefore, even more powerful in the human world. During the 1600s, Japanese textile factories bred cats to control mice infestations in silk factories. Soon, the surrounding towns were overrun with feral cats. This unwelcome overabundance spurred the rumor that the Bakeneko may kill its human guardian in order to take over the household.

Perhaps the struggle with the Bakeneko boils down to control. Cutting kittens' tails and discarding elderly cats are horrible practices, without a doubt. Their desire for revenge is understandable. Luckily, in modern times, the Bakeneko and Nekomata have lost their evil edge and are popularized as cute kitty personalities in manga, anime, movies, and books. If only all human power struggles could be resolved with cuteness!

DAWON

This sacred cat is part tiger and part lion, known in the animal world as a liger, or *Ghatokbahini*. Dawon was a gift to the Indian goddess Parvati, a spouse of Shiva, also known as the Daughter of the Mountain. This Hindu goddess of sexuality, war, and transformation was also sometimes called Uma, Gauri, or Durga.

When riding astride this magnificent creature, she burst onto the battlefield in an impressive scene. Dawon enhanced her own image as both a divine being and a conquering force, which was intimidating to her foes. The duo became an impressive team because Parvati could wield ten weapons at a time while the liger helped her attack her enemies with his large teeth and long claws.

How we present ourselves to the world impacts our effectiveness. By showing her agility with vast weaponry and facing her challengers alongside a powerful ally, the goddess drew down her own Divine Feline Energy. Her determination to prevail meant bringing her full force into battle as well as gathering support from a trusted friend, which is a great example for us when facing upsets in our own mortal lives.

— HAETAE —

In Korean mythology, Haetae, sometimes written as Hae-chi, is depicted with a lion's body, a unicorn's horn, and armor-like scales. Haetae is an official symbol in Seoul where he appears on many buildings, has statues in his honor, and is considered a protector against natural disasters, such as fires or floods. Although his appearance is a bizarre mash-up from various creatures, Haetae is considered playful and friendly in Korea and is seen as a guardian of the people and a beloved deity. However, in other parts of Asia, Haetae may be considered ferocious and one to be feared.

For example, in China he is known by Xiezhi, where he is a symbol of judgment. He is called upon as a moral mediator to determine who is right or wrong and will ram the guilty party with his sharp horn. The image of Xiezhi serves as a reminder of upholding ethical conduct and suffering the consequences, as does the figurine of the Lady of Justice holding the balancing scales in Western culture. In Japan, this lion-unicorn hybrid is called Kaichi, where he is also an enforcer of justice, impaling the guilty with his horn.

When we are wronged by a person or situation, it is natural to feel the urge to react. However, the lesson of the Haetae is to wait and let the sharp horn of Karma deliver justice in due time. Meanwhile, stay focused on your own evolution.

JINHUA CAT

· · · · · · · · · ·

The strange tale of the mystical Jinhua Cat demon is somewhat like the Japanese Bakeneko. It begins with a paranormal creature who poses as a normal house cat. Once this cunning creature has spent at least three years living within a family, it transforms into its true magical nature. This change is observed when the cat begins to make its way to the rooftop every night where it sits, mouth agape, absorbing the soft glow of the moon.

As it connects with the moon, channeling the dark side of Divine Feline Energy, and its ethereal powers get stronger, the Jinhua Cat leaves domesticity behind and hides in the woods during the day. At night, it can use its powers to take an enchanting human form—male or female—to seduce its victim and be invited into their home. Once inside, it can bring illness and death to the inhabitants and take over the family home as its lair.

The only way to be cured from the curse of this spirit is for it to be caught and its flesh roasted over an open fire. The afflicted person, or persons, must then eat the meat, and only then do they have a chance to recover from the illness inflicted by this cat-shaped demon. Obviously, this is not a concept embraced by cat lovers today even if it were to undo an evil enchantment.

This story can be a warning to get to know people well before divulging too much personal information or opening one's heart. Knowing who we invite into our homes or into our lives helps to avoid potential betrayal down the road. While a new friend, lover, or work colleague may bring joy initially, take time to evaluate whether to trust them with secrets or cherished dreams.

KASHA

Sometimes depicted as large as a human, this mischievous cat is a *yōkai*—or supernatural being, monster, or demon—in Japanese folklore. The Kasha are human size or larger, and usually show themselves only under cover of darkness or in stormy weather. This fiery feline can walk through rain, throwing lightning rods and flames, and can set things ablaze even in the midst of a downpour. They are definitely not the cuddly kitties we are used to!

These creepy cat demons had a purpose for walking among humans—to steal the dead. Some Kasha would disguise themselves as house cats to avoid being caught. They'd then hide in the rafters during a wake or funeral ceremony and leap down to snatch the body. Then it would either take its true form and eat the body as a tasty treat or carry it to the Underworld for judgment. If a person was taken by the cat, he or she would not be able to enter the afterlife. All this said, was the Kasha really so bad? He only took wicked people, so becoming prey might have been a fit fate for them, after all.

In order to protect the dead, whether they were good or bad, the priests sometimes held two funeral services. In the first one, they filled the coffin with rocks to trick the Kasha, hoping it would take the rocks instead of the body. The word *kasha* can also mean "fire chariot," given their tendency to wheel the corpses away with fire bolts flashing around them. To scare them away, the funeral goers sometimes also played loud instruments.

Perhaps the Kasha encourages people to consider how they are living their lives. What would be your judgment at the end of your life? Are you moving through the world as the person you want to be? Are you doing bad things to attract the attention of a corpse-robbing demon, or are you channeling your best and kindest self?

LI SHOU

The most revered cat deity in ancient Chinese beliefs was Li Shou. This majestic feline is of such importance that she is even mentioned in the Chinese Book of Rites. Elegant, beautiful, and kind, she possessed the ability to not only communicate with the elements and other gods, but she could also channel Divine Feline Energy to grant favors for the people on Earth. In short, she was a goddess in her own right as well as a conduit between this world and the heavens.

Her long whiskers, thick fur, bushy tail, and regal demeanor also made her especially aesthetically pleasing. Just looking upon her image was considered good fortune, and figurines in her likeness were kept on public altars and in sacred meditation areas in private homes. The popularity of the thousands of guardian lions around China could also be attributed to people's love for this sacred feline.

Li Shou was believed to bless harvests and, therefore, was revered by farmers and the communities fed by their crops. They would pray to her and offer gifts that any beloved kitty would enjoy. These could include colorful ribbons or delectable morsels of choice bits of meat. People who cared for feral cats and kept feline fur babies in their homes as pets were especially favored by Li Shou.

This goddess was also a protector of families and a mother figure, even ensuring that they would have abundant crops by driving mice and pests out of the fields. Li Shou was also a favorite companion of the benevolent and beautiful human goddess Miao-shan, who was known for her compassion and often depicted with an ethereal cat by her side.

Cats and cat deities have been part of Chinese culture for millennia and were especially popular during the Song dynasty. During that period, cats were almost on the level of concubines since they were often given gifts and pampered. There are also famous poems about cats from that era.

The elegant cat not only benefits the person who loves them by bringing them joy and good company, they also provide important services. Through their hunting skills, homes are kept pest-free, which reduces risk of illness from rodent droppings and fleas. Not to mention, having a clever and gorgeous cat as a housemate might encourage us all to be a little more conscious of our own appearance.

MANEKI NEKO

More than a souvenir shop trinket or colorful cat figurine, the Japanese Maneki Neko, or "beckoning cat," has deep cultural roots and significance. Cats are well loved in Japan, and a Maneki Neko sitting by the door of a shop or home invites good fortune. It is said that the Maneki Neko should always be displayed in the busiest areas of a home or business because people-watching is one of the favorite pastimes of a curious cat.

The tale behind this famous cat recounts a clever feline who enticed a lord into a temple from across the road during a massive thunderstorm by raising its arm and beckoning him in. This saved the man from being struck by lightning. The lord, named Naotaka Ii, later paid for the building of the Goto-kuji temple in the Setagaya ward of Tokyo and the magical cat roamed the lush grounds. After the cat's death, the Shofuku-den was added to enshrine the kitty who had been named Maneki Neko. To this day, people visit the site to ask for blessings for their families, including wealth and happiness. Aside from the shrine, there are thousands of lucky cat figurines, large and small, dotting the gardens throughout the property.

Something that many people may not realize is that Maneki Neko effigies are quite individualized, as there are specific meanings to their colors and other pertinent symbols painted onto them. Tricolored calico or pure white are the most popular coats on Maneki Neko statues. Calico is thought to bring luck and white denotes pure joy. Gold figures are also widely displayed and, as one might guess, these represent financial abundance, especially when placed on the west side of the building. Red cat statues most often relate to health and longevity, and these are usually in the entranceway of a home or hospital to keep germs at bay. Pink correlates to romance, blue enhances intelligence and cunning, and green brings tranquility.

The paws on the Maneki Neko also have meaning. If the paw is a back-and-forth wagging one, the closer it reaches toward the cat's ear, the more riches will come to the observer.

If the right hand is waving, the cat god is a male and attracts financial success. If the left hand is up, the statuette is a female and will invite more people into one's life, perhaps a new lover. One with both hands raised will attract money and enhance personal relationships. Sometimes, the cats are holding or wearing special items. Some have bibs, which mean they are protective totems. Some are holding coins symbolizing wealth. A fish in hand displays vigor, a gemstone is for wisdom, a gourd will ward off evil spirits, and a daikon radish brings good luck.

Enthusiasts of Maneki Neko in the United States can visit the Lucky Cat Museum in Cincinnati, Ohio, which boasts a couple thousand figurines on display. And anyone who is hoping to bring more money, success, or love into their lives can buy the kind of ceramic good luck cat that most fits their desire. When placing the Maneki Neko in your home, business, or in your own meditation space, visualize the riches flowing to you through the power of Divine Feline Energy.

NIAN

· · · · · · · · · ·

Lunar New Year, or Chinese New Year, is often associated with the color red. It is also traditional to set off fireworks. While the festival color and little explosions add liveliness to celebrations, there is another root for these customs.

An ancient Chinese tale speaks of a fierce water-dwelling creature called a Nian, which had a slithery body and a lion's head with a sharp horn. The cornet was not merely decorative but used to attack its prey or adversary. Although the beast was believed to live at the bottom of the sea, on the last day of the year it would swim to shore to fill its belly with humans and their livestock. Therefore, on the eve of every lunar new year, the people would lock up their animals and lock themselves in their houses.

Finally, they had had enough of living in fear on this night of celebration, so a village elder decided to take matters into his own hands and rid them of the leonine demon. The old man dressed in bright red garments to give himself an otherworldly look and hid himself in the bushes as night began to fall. Just as the Nian crept into the village to begin its yearly plunder, the man let off many brightly colored, loud fireworks. Anyone with a cat for a pet knows that they do not like loud sounds, so this was an effective tool. The Nian stopped in its tracks, trembled with fear, and ran off, not to return. According to the story, this

is what led to the yearly tradition of red decorations and crack-
ling skyward displays.

This creative resolution shows how one person's ingenu-
ity saved a town from harassment by the Nian. Not only did
the old man's clever thinking stop the creature from ruining
the town's special night, he did so without shedding a drop of
blood. Maybe we can also think of ingenious yet harmless ways
to beat an adversary, resulting in a win for all involved. Wouldn't
it be wonderful if human clashes could end with fireworks and
a big party?

PATRIPARAN

This enchanting cat from Indian folklore was popularized in a famous book, *Histoire des Chats (History of Cats)*, by the eighteenth-century French writer and scholar Francois Augustin de Paradis de Moncrif about a competition between a brahmin and a penitent in King Salangham's court.

The king lusted after a particular sacred flower that only existed in the heavens, beyond human reach. The penitent insisted that he could task the enchanted cat Patriparan with obtaining the flower and when the king agreed to allow him to try this, the penitent whispered into the ear of the feline who set out upon his quest.

Once Patriparan arrived at the enchanted realm, however, one of the most beautiful goddesses fell in love with the cat and insisted that he stay with her. She struck a deal with the king that if he allowed her to keep the lustrous cat with her for three centuries, she would return him. During this time, the humans would not age at all. Everyone agreed to humor the goddess, and lived for three hundred years.

When the time was up, the sky became brilliant and Patriparan floated back down to Earth on a kitty throne made of the sacred flowers. He also brought a branch full of blooms as a gift for the king. One wonders whether the magical cat would have preferred to stay in the heavens, adored by a goddess who spoiled him with love and sat him upon his own throne—alas, he was not asked his opinion on the matter.

What is remarkable about this story is that the goddess did not simply take the cat. Instead, although she held the power as a divine being, she offered a deal to the mortals, giving them something they found valuable—three hundred extra years of life—in thanks. Expressing appreciation can seem like a lost art in today's busy and often unappreciative society. Wouldn't it be splendid to offer tokens of appreciation—even a thankful word—when someone brings us joy or grants us a favor?

PHI CHA KLA

This Thai demon is a dark-colored cat whose hair grows back to front. His red eyes flash with fear if he sees a human, and he disappears into his dingy underground lair if one comes near. If a human touches—or even makes eye contact with—this ghostly nocturnal feline, it is feared that they will soon die.

Stories in Thai folklore often have a lesson at their core. The anecdotes in this part of the world are often rooted in Buddhism, so there is an element of wisdom that can be shared, too. So, what could be the moral of the story of mysterious Phi Cha Kla?

A sense of community is integral to one's well-being, and we know that people who live the longest are not isolationists, like this sad demon cat. Rather than withdrawing in hard times and hiding out in our proverbial lairs, we need to reach out to trusted family members or friends. Likewise, if someone in our circle seems a bit off, we could ask if they are in need of emotional support. Giving compassion to ourselves as well as to others is a foundational Buddhist belief, and maybe Phi Cha Kla is a reminder of how *not* to live our lives.

SASHT

· · · · · · · · · ·

Also called Shashthi, this Indian goddess has a complicated relationship with a magical cat. She is sometimes intertwined with other cat deities because, like so many of them, she is associated with childbirth. She has either kind or selfish qualities, depending on the story and the time period in which her story is told.

This goddess likely originates in the Goa area, where Sasht is invoked on the sixth day after the birth of a child. The story goes that, centuries ago, a pregnant woman stole food from a local merchant. When caught, she blamed it on a cat who was friendly with Sasht. The poor cat was pelted with stones by the shopkeeper who had, until then, been feeding it occasional scraps. Having humanlike feelings of vengeance and with the aid of Sasht, the hungry cat then stalked the pregnant woman and stole her baby and each subsequent child, taking them as servants to the goddess.

The woman finally prayed to the goddess to forgive her unjust accusation. In a dream, she was instructed to sculpt the figure of a cat from rice and place it alongside a drawing of the goddess herself. Then the woman should honor her with prayers and offerings of incense and flowers. She should also fast for six days, and on the last day break the fast by drinking milk and eating fruit. Upon the completion of this ritual, her consequent babies would be blessed with good health and long life.

This strange tale can be seen as how to atone for doing wrong and, particularly, for causing harm to another being. While it is difficult to want to punish a pregnant woman taking food if she is hungry, blaming her crime on an innocent party was the larger offense. The cat was physically punished and cast out when it had done nothing wrong. Perhaps the moral of this anecdote is that when we do wrong, rather than scapegoating, we should own our actions and show true remorse.

SINH

This angelic, sacred cat was a loyal companion to the head Buddhist priest Mun-Ha in Burma. They both lived at the Temple of Lao-Tsun where at least one hundred white cats with yellow eyes lived and were considered spiritual guardians. These cats were said to represent the souls of the priests who had died and were awaiting reincarnation.

The goddess of that temple was Tsun-Kyan-Kse, who oversaw the souls of these priests and protected them as they meditated in cat form until they were born into new human bodies to return even more enlightened than before. This luminescent deity wore long golden robes and was known for her illustrious bright blue eyes.

Sinh was the constant companion of his holy friend, so he was present when intruders broke into the temple one day hoping to steal the golden statue of their goddess among other valuable items. Mun-Ha tried fighting off the robbers and was mortally injured in the process. The sacred cat went into a violent frenzy, hissing at the murderers and calling to all the other white feline guardians to help scare them away. The cats fell upon the evil men in a swarm, clawed them, and managed to close the doors of the temple as the robbers ran away.

Filled with grief, Sinh lay next to the dying priest and placed his paws upon him to comfort him as he took his last breaths. As the cats gathered around their beloved human friend, Sinh looked to the goddess for strength. As he did so, his fur turned a golden hue like her robes and his yellow eyes became a stunning sapphire blue, like those of the goddess. His little paws, where they touched his friend, remained pure white.

The bereaved cat sat upon Mun-Ha's throne for seven days and then he also died. When he passed over to the afterlife, he found his friend Mun-Ha and guided his spirit to paradise to await his reincarnation. The other temple cats prayed and grieved the loss of Sinh for the next seven days, and then the goddess descended, turning all their fur golden, their eyes blue, and kept their paws white.

Love and loyalty are on full display in this story. Being part of a community means protecting those we love, and knowing we have true allies in them are some of the greatest riches we can hope for in life. As a reminder of this sentiment, the purebred Birman cats, also called the Sacred Cats of Burma, have white paws and blue eyes to this day.

WAGHOBA

· · · · · · · · ·

People creating communities in areas previously only inhabited by wild animals must find ways to coexist. Unfortunately, many humans feel it is their right to kill the beasts who live in the jungles, forests, and waters near where a new town is expanding. With villages come farms and livestock, and the wildcats in that area do not understand that those animals are off-limits to them.

Waghoba is depicted as either a leopard or a tiger, depending upon the teller, and is the central figure in a story about being true to one's nature. It is his natural instinct to eat the goats and other animals people brought along for their own use but, in the tale, the people rise up to seek revenge on the confused cat. Why were they so upset for his enjoying the meal he believes they set out for him?

Finally, Waghoba's mother comes to the rescue and negotiates a peaceful outcome for all. The people would hold the annual festival of Waghbaras and sacrifice an animal for the big cats to feast upon. In return, the felines would steer clear of their settlement the rest of the time.

Imagine if all the people in the world decided to recognize the individuality of the other, and respect their needs alongside their own. This festival is an example of the art of compromise and mutual awareness. As the human population continues to explode and we encroach upon previously untamed land, being conscious that the animals who live there must also eat and find safe spaces to raise their young would benefit the natural spaces and all of their valued inhabitants.

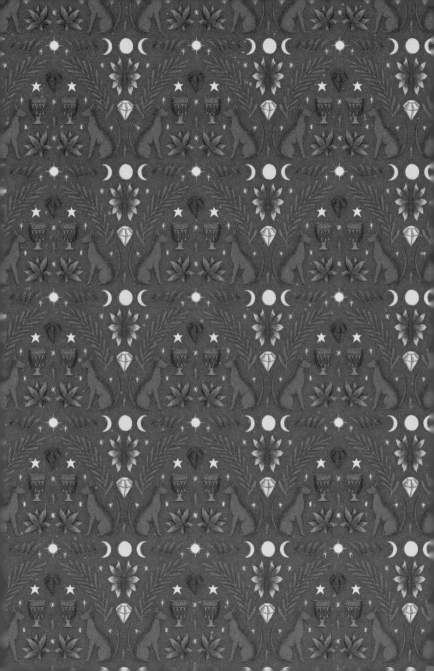

EUROPE

Stories of creatures with mythological ties are abundant among the people who settled the mass of land we call Europe, today. No matter the origin of the group—descendants from Greek and Roman soldiers' conquests, wandering Celtic tribes, offspring from plundering Viking clans, or any combination of people who created communities across the expanses from Spain to Croatia—animals figured prominently in their beliefs.

Magical beings included banshees, basilisks, unicorns, phoenixes, dragons, canines, and felines of all sorts. We know that cats are the unequivocal spirit animal of the goddesses, particularly the deities of fertility and war as this book highlights across cultures and centuries. Cats are wild, free, and only tamed when they wish to be. They are godlike if for nothing but this liberty of spirit alone.

Cats were likely brought to the Mediterranean region by the Phoenicians as early as 500 BCE. Their civilization was centered in modern-day Lebanon, and we have already explored the fondness ancient Arabic cultures had for cats and feline deities. Cats were also essential to ships as they would kill stowaway rodents who threatened the sailors' stores of food on board.

The felines proliferated and many distinct and beautiful cat breeds would evolve over the ages, finding their place in communities as well as folklore. Even today, particular cat breeds are associated with parts of Europe. For example, the Norwegian Forest Cats are large and fluffy creatures, much like the fearsome bearded Vikings of yore with whom they shared space. These cats have a collar of thick fur and tufts of hair growing from their ears. Their size—larger than most small dogs—and their bushy, silken coats protect them through long, dark, snowy winters.

Other European cats have been bred for aesthetic reasons. The British Shorthair has alluring round eyes and dense soft fur, often smoky gray. The Chartreux in France looks very similar. They are elegant little fellows and fit the aesthetic of the refined upper classes in both of those countries. The Ukrainian Levkoy has a distinct appearance with its folded ears and a body with very little fur. They have long faces and look somewhat like the Egyptian cats depicted on ancient burial sites. In short, the cat breeds are as diverse as the languages and cultures across Europe itself, and so are their feline deities and demons.

To this day, visiting Greece means encountering many cats. They abound in the streets of Athens, and many kitty colonies are cared for by people living in their neighborhoods. This goes for neighboring Turkey as well. Appreciation for felines dates to ancient Greek civilization, particularly the era when many of the people began migrating to cat-worshipping Egypt, about 600 BCE.

Upon return to Greece, members of cat cults shared the felinistic religions with their countrymen. In many cases, new and old gods were melded together, as we see very clearly in the feline god lineage of Egyptian (Bastet) to Greek (Artemis) to Roman (Diana).

As people moved across Europe, paganism mixed with Christianity while Islam and Judaism made cultural ripples, as well. Arabic culture particularly touched southern Europe as seen in the stunning Alhambra in Spain, which is home to hundreds of cats to this day. Petting the wandering kitties in the palace gardens is one of the attractions there for cat lovers.

The Greeks so loved their cats that—per the famed historian Herodotus—when a feline pet passed away, the entire family shaved their eyebrows in mourning, a period that would last until the hair grew back. Dionysus, the god of wine and revelry, rode a magical leopard. Galinthias was turned into a cat for helping bring Hercules into the world, and Hecate, the goddess of witchcraft, regularly took cat form herself. In short, Greek legends are rife with cat worship and lore.

The Romans also had an attachment to cats, and they especially respected their prowess as hunters. They saw them as tireless and cunning when attacking their prey, much like the virtues of a solid Roman soldier in battle. In Greco-Roman art, cats appeared on vases, carved into stone slabs and feline-shaped amulets, and even appeared on ancient coins.

Roman towns were well organized, and the townspeople were adept at storing food for lean times. Obviously, cats were helpful in keeping mice at bay. Various rodents also chewed through leather and wood, thereby damaging armor and military equipment, and little pests were already starting to be recognized for spreading disease. Cats became mascots to armies, pets to families, and were incorporated into Roman mythology.

The Romans also included cats in their mythical symbolism because they were the embodiment of independence and freedom, values held dear in Roman culture. In fact, cats were the only animals allowed inside Roman temples. The goddess Libertas is associated with freedom-loving felines.

Cats were loved by all Romans but said to be especially enjoyed by women due to their playfulness and companionship when their men were on long military journeys. Cat lovers know that pet kitties are intuitive beings and seem to sense when their human companion could benefit from a cuddle. The Roman ladies also strolled around town with their prize pets on leashes. In Pompeii, the skeleton of a woman holding a cat was uncovered during excavation. Obviously, this was a beloved family pet, and one wonders if she gave her life trying to save it, or if they were taken by the hellish volcanic eruption together.

In Scandinavia, especially in Norse mythology, cats play a large role. Freya, yet another goddess of love, fertility, and war, had two magical felines who pulled her chariot across the sky. By some accounts, they were as big as horses and had massive wings. The cats were gifted to her by the war god Thor, who was also associated with cat magic. In one account, he disguised himself as a cat to sneak into the lair of Thrym in order to retrieve his enchanted hammer. Incidentally, giant, flying dragon-like mythical cats, like Freya's, make appearances in other global folktales as well.

The idea of a cat's color determining whether it brings good or bad luck is attributed to European tales. This unfair measuring stick of "good" or "bad" cats continues today in many countries, including the United States. Animal shelters have recorded a black cat bias whereby darker-colored kitties are the last to be adopted, and therefore have the highest euthanasia rates. Interestingly, though, black cats are considered good luck in parts of Great Britain and even Japan.

Starting around the fifth century, Christians spread across Europe and sought to replace nature-based religions, which included the worship of animal gods, with their own. They implemented legislation against pagan rituals, used violence to intimidate native people, and created smear campaigns against the very cats who had been associated with gods and goddesses in the ancient civilizations. Instead, they transmuted these revered animals into evil accomplices, aiding witches and monsters in European tales. Pagan groups had previously seen trees, animals, and the elements as having their own consciousness, power, and holiness whereas Christianity forced the idea of only one omnipotent god who created—and dominated—everything.

Priests spread false rumors that cats' teeth were venomous and that their fur was lethal if it touched human skin. While some people could have had cat allergies, the church took advantage of sneezing and wheezing as proof that the mere breath of a feline destroyed human lungs. Priests even flat out accused cats and cat lovers as being one with the devil and began exterminating them—both the cats and their so-called sorcerer friends. In sadistic rituals, cats were systematically murdered as the newly faithful looked on.

In an ironic twist, over time so many cats were killed during these dark times that rats and mice ran rampant. The vermin spread disease throughout Europe, and it is believed that a few centuries later a dearth of cats led to an accelerated spread of the plague. If only cats had maintained their place in society as helpers in pest control, the unrelenting terror of illness and death could have possibly been avoided.

There was some vindication for cats in the age of the Enlightenment. By the nineteenth century, our friendly floofs had again been elevated to the status of pampered pets. Another religious movement—the Protestant Reformation—is credited with breaking the dark spell of the Catholic priests and their many ridiculous superstitions surrounding nature and animals. People were encouraged to use their own minds to determine what was favorable and what was evil.

When British Queen Victoria became interested in cats through the archeological findings in Egypt, she adopted two Blue Persian kittens who were treated as exaltedly as any member of her court. This fondness of cats by the monarch made having a cat as a pet favored among the nobility, and once the British upper classes began to see cats as worthy companions, the fashion of bringing them into one's home spread across the pond to the United States.

When writer Sarah Josepha Hale wrote a piece for *Godey's Lady's Book* about cats being fine pets for everyday people, not only British nobility, their popularity soared even higher. Louis A. Godey's monthly magazine in the mid-1800s set the lifestyle standards for people "keeping up with the Joneses" in his day. Among the many other popularizations that came about due to the periodical is the tradition of having a Christmas tree in one's home each holiday season as well as advocating for women's rights and celebrating Thanksgiving. Happily, by endorsing the trend of adopting kitties, the joy of cats as pets has become commonplace since it was touted in the journal. Cat companions are as naturally incorporated into our lives as is any other family member the world over.

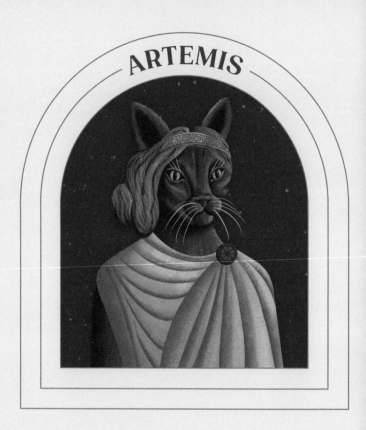

ARTEMIS

Artemis is the Greek equivalent to the Egyptian Bastet and Roman Diana. She was often called the Mistress of Animals since she was frequently depicted surrounded by feathered, scaled, winged, and furry friends, and cats in particular. She would dance through forests, mountains, and waterways with her entourage of nymphs and naiads, sometimes taking a slinky cat form herself. Artemis was sometimes referred to as the Goddess of the Tree Cult as well as Lady of the Lake. She was the guardian of lush, wild places filled with greenery, flowers, sentient beings of all kinds, and bountiful fresh springs.

Her cult followers associate her with lascivious love affairs and—the logical follow-on to love affairs in a pre–birth control world—procreation. Cats were kept near pregnant women to shoo harmful spirits away from newborns. Artemis was considered a protector of babies, both humans and animals. She was also a patron of hunters, so we can assume that she was yet another goddess who turned the wheel of life and death.

The worship of Artemis flourished in Crete as well as the mainland during the pre-Hellenic era. Over time, of course, she was combined with other deities within and outside of Greek culture. Her temple, whose remains are in modern-day Turkey, was once one of the Seven Wonders of the World.

Any goddess of fertility and physical love is an usher of new beginnings. This could be a new stage of life—adolescence, adulthood, midlife, retirement, or becoming a respected elder. All stages of life have value and each new beginning brings exciting ways to express it. Perhaps connecting with Artemis will expedite the blossoming of a new project, an intriguing lover, or entering evolution along your own spiritual path.

ASLAN

As overlord of the magical kingdom of Narnia and gentle protector of the four children who entered his land through an enchanted wardrobe, Aslan is a modern feline deity who deserves his place among the other gods and goddesses of yore. He is known to most of us as the loving, godlike father figure in British author C. S. Lewis's book series *The Chronicles of Narnia*. This enchanting series of books left a mark on young readers since their publishing in 1950.

Called The Great Lion, Aslan created a kingdom that encompasses all the worlds that exist. Legend says that he sang the world into existence with his powerful roar, and when he is not helping the creatures who live within the worlds he created, he dwells beyond the rising sun. Aslan represents the embodiment of goodness and protects Narnians against the evil White Witch, who personifies deception, cruelty, and greed.

Aslan comes to the aid of the children in their darkest moments. For example, even after The Great Lion warned the children to avoid the evil White Witch, Edmund selfishly betrayed him when he was offered a chance to satisfy his own greed. His weakness placed him in a compromising position, at the mercy of the sorceress who insisted that the only way she'd let the child go was if Aslan offered his life in place of Edmund's. Aslan sacrificed himself to save him, the ultimate act of unconditional love. As a magical being, Aslan soon arose again from the stone slab on which he was killed, forgiving all that happened, and continuing to guide his Narnian subjects with kindness.

In addition to the story of self-sacrifice to save his child, Aslan is also referred to as the Son of the Emperor Over the Sea. It was easy to understand that the author intended for this supernatural cat to be reminiscent of Jesus, the Christian god, who sacrificed himself to free humans from their own sins. And, like other gods, Aslan will endure as part of modern mythology for many years to come.

Mustering forgiveness for those who have wronged us or taken us for granted is a deep act of compassion because it affords the perpetrators an opportunity for growth if they recognize it. Releasing past pain also frees us and allows us to keep moving forward in our own evolution. The idea of being reborn each day allows us to focus on the good things to come rather than dwelling on bygone unhappiness.

CAT SÍ

Related to the legend of the Cat Sith is the Cat Sí, also known as the King of Cats. This creature was more faerie than animal, and like the witchy Cat Sith, it had a fondness for snagging the souls of freshly dead humans. Because of this nefarious hobby, cats—especially black ones—were chased out of graveyards and were not let near mortuaries. They could be appeased with saucers of milk though, and this exchange kept peace in the town. Most agreed that was a small price to pay.

However, there were outliers. One old man considered the tradition of leaving offerings for magical cats to be ridiculous nonsense. No matter how much his neighbors begged him to oblige them in following tradition to protect their crops and keep dark faeries at bay, he was not going to be manipulated. Instead, he came up with a nasty plan.

One night he poisoned a saucer of milk, left it out, and went to bed. In the wee hours there was a knock at his door, and when he opened it, he found a cat there, dying. Elated, he jumped over the cat and headed to his local pub to raise a glass to himself and boast about his wicked accomplishment.

In a dark corner, a black cat was curled up dozing near the fire. When he heard the slurring man, swaying back and forth, bragging that he killed the Cat Sí, the pub cat leaped to his feet and shouted in a booming human voice, "That was my father. Now I am King of the Cats!" The enchanted feline demon then threw himself upon the man and clawed him viciously. Yowling, he chased the man who was found dead in a field the next morning. From then on, in that village, you can bet that there were saucers of milk aplenty.

The moral of this tale could be that we don't have to do harm to those who we do not find to our liking. We can act with mindfulness rather than reacting out of exasperation. Doing no harm is more enlightened than being right.

CAT SITH

In Celtic legends, these sorcerer cats were guardians of the Underworld. Some say they hailed from the Scottish Highlands, and others say they were from Ireland. They are likely from both, and perhaps roamed around even more of the Celtic areas.

These spooky kitties had beautiful black coats, usually with a white tuft on their chests. Some could even sprout wings, as they were considered part faerie. Their name comes from two Gaelic words—*cait* meaning "cat" and *sith*, which translates to "faeries." They were linked with witches and dark faeries and considered duplicitous.

The magical felines were tricksters who could transform back and forth into humans nine times, and on the ninth turn they would be cats forever. This could be where the idea of a cat having nine lives originated.

When in cat form, the Cat Sith would slink around freshly dead bodies to slyly steal their souls and take them back to their enchanted island in the dark world as trophies. In order to keep these evil spirits away from loved ones as they passed to the next world, family and friends would stand guard all night and play music and dance. This was meant to scare the nasty faeries away and became known as what we now call a wake.

But the cat demons also had a benevolent side. If befriended, these supernatural cats could speak to humans in their own language and tell the future. This could have an obvious advantage, so to stay on the Cat Sith's good side, villagers would leave treats at their doors on Samhain, the Pagan predecessor to Halloween. Farm folk who forgot the milk on the sacred eve would soon find their cows' udders went dry.

Does it pay to "dance with the devil"? Befriending a duplicitous character may seem like a power move but, ultimately, someone who betrays others will likely do the same to you. Learning the art of diplomacy and sidestepping the underhanded folks who get ahead at all costs will help you avoid getting on the bad side of someone you'd rather not even know.

DIANA

Perhaps the most commanding Roman goddess, Diana is the daughter of Jupiter and the equivalent to Bastet in Egypt and Artemis in Greece. As a patron of the hunt, Diana is associated with many animals. She could transform into a cat and hide herself in the shadows of the moon to look at the people on Earth the way a mother would gaze upon her sleeping child.

She, too, was associated with both death and new life. She was often invoked when people went hunting so she could help them kill a deer or other such animal. Warriors also made offerings to her when going into battle.

As a fertility goddess, Diana would be depicted as a gentle mother figure with multiple breasts, which echoes a mother cat who feeds her kittens from many teats. She was called upon by members of her cult for help with conceiving a child as well as support during all stages of pregnancy. She was also asked to hold sacred spiritual space for a fragile baby's safe entrance to the world.

Associated with the wonders of nature, Diana's followers often worshipped her by holding celebrations in the woods. Diana was also the patron of the lower classes of society, including Roman slaves. Her priests were often former slaves who escaped or fought their way to freedom.

The ultimate symbol of feminine power, Diana reflects nurturing, sustenance, and battle. She is at once fierce and kind, fearsome and helpful. We all have multiple facets to our personalities and exploring the nuances of our relationships will help us bring forth the most enlightened parts of ourselves.

GALINTHIAS

Galinthias was the midwife who delivered the god Hercu-les. Her assistance with this event angered the goddess Hera, who was both the sister and wife of unfaithful Zeus. Her phi-landering husband impregnated a mortal woman, Princess Alc-mene, so upon learning of this pending love child, Hera flew into a jealous rage and plotted to kill the baby. Galinthias was the princess's lady-in-waiting, so when she heard of the god-dess's evil plan, she helped Alcmene save her son.

Hera set a spell that delayed the birth of the baby, making the mother suffer for several days in excruciating pain. Finally, with the help of divine intervention, Galinthias aided in breaking the curse, delivering a healthy baby boy.

The enraged goddess sought revenge upon Galinthias for foiling her plan by turning her into a black cat. Luckily for the kindhearted and brave midwife, she was taken in by Hecate—the powerful goddess of witchcraft—who was thrilled to have the magical feline as her companion. Though black cats are considered holy in some cultures, this story could be the origin of their association with witches and the dark arts.

Despite what befell Galinthias, she made the most of the situation. Hera sought to make her miserable by turning her into a cat, but instead Galinthias's resilience helped her find a positive solution. Her new alliance with Hecate gave her powers beyond what she had as a human and also protection from the magic that surrounded the witch. Sometimes what seems like a dead end is a fresh start with unexpected benefits.

GRIMALKIN

· · · · · · · · · ·

The Grimalkin is a magical gray cat from Celtic lore that was so famous it has been featured in many works of art, including a mention by Shakespeare in his play *Macbeth*. The adjacent word *graymalkin* is an ancient term for a cat. The word is comprised of *gray* and *malkin*, and the latter word dates to the thirteenth century, referring to a servant and, in some cases, a promiscuous woman.

The Grimalkin was seen as a witch's helper, so it was particularly disturbing for the god-fearing people who already suspected that a feline skulking outside a church indicated devilish forces nearby. Some even believed that the Grimalkin was actually a witch in disguise.

This troublesome nonsense became an excuse for members of the clergy, or of European high society, to accuse women who kept cats of being involved with sorcery and other magical mischief. During the sixteenth to eighteenth centuries, this misogynistic persecution extended its long arm to North America, too, where women accused of witchcraft were burned alive, drowned, or flogged to death. Their furry companions were considered devilish helpers, and sometimes killed as well.

Obviously, the lesson here is not to let group hysteria take over your own common sense. Whether a religious group, peer pressure from friends, or even your own family, if what others say doesn't add up, it is not necessary to join in with them. Imagine how many innocent women's lives could have been saved if friends and neighbors refused to accept the false paranoia and panic when people turned on those around them.

JÓLAKÖTTURINN

Also known as the Yule Cat, this monstrous black demon from Icelandic folklore dates back to the Dark Ages. The foul feline could be considered a wicked sort of Christmas elf because he showed up around the holidays to enforce good behavior and oversee tradition. The Jólakötturinn was said to be the size of a house, and as he prowled around the villages, he would seek out and then eat children who were not wearing at least one item of new clothing, per holiday custom.

Children would earn these new clothes by finishing their chores before the Christmas celebrations. This scary story was perhaps told to make new school clothes seem at least as valuable as the latest cool toy to tiny tots. If they received new clothes, the child was assumed to have been well-behaved. Children who did not get them were considered naughty, and so they were subjected to becoming a meal for the demon cat. As if the Jólakötturinn wasn't enough, his troll companions— Grýla, Leppalúði, and their thirteen children—were collectively known as the Yule Lads, and they would help sniff out the unruly kiddos.

This tale was passed down through many generations, and in 1932, the Jólakötturinn appeared in a book of holiday poems called the *Jólin Koma*. In 1987, Icelandic pop sensation Björk adapted the poem into a song. While this tale enforces adhering to the rules or suffering the consequences, for some people breaking tradition means being able to walk their own path in life. Perhaps releasing the deep-rooted fear of not doing as others wish is the key to achieving an important personal goal.

KETTA

Ancient Vikings believed the ketta were fierce cat spirits who could shape-shift into women in order to carry out their clandestine plans. Sometimes they stopped halfway, appearing as half woman, half cat. The word *ketta* means "she cat," but it can also mean "evil spirit" in some Scandinavian languages.

The ketta are talented at pretending to be human, which makes them particularly dangerous. They can be almost undetectable shape-shifters apart from the long, sharp claws that stretch out from their fingers. This is the one aspect of their cat form they cannot change. These fearsome creatures appear in various legends in old European stories such as the Anglo-Saxon poem *Beowulf* in which the mother of the monster Grendel is a ketta.

The ketta are also associated with Freya, the beautiful Norse goddess of fertility, lust, and warfare. Like a cat, she is seductive and sly and can also be extremely aggressive to those who threaten her. Thor, the god of warfare and thunder, was charmed by the effervescent Freya and gifted her two magic giant cats, which she named Bygul and Triegul. The pair were as big as horses with massive wings so they could pull Freya's fiery chariot across the sky.

Transformation is part of nearly every magical tale and is part of every human life at some point. We can also draw upon Divine Feline Energy to channel the inspiration to turn obstacles into opportunities. Completing that process requires one part intention and one part action. When we eventually create a solution on the other side of a challenge, it can feel like we are soaring beyond what we even thought possible.

LIBERTAS

Despite having a large population of enslaved people in their society, the ancient Romans held personal autonomy and independence as high values. Hence, Libertas was a popular goddess. She was an elegant symbol of freedom and usually appeared holding a scepter, a symbol of divine power. It is believed that the modern-day Statue of Liberty, holding a torch to light the path to a new life for the encumbered masses, was inspired by this image.

Libertas was worshipped by those wishing for freedom as much as those who already had it. As any cat lover knows, they are the quintessential animals of living by one's own rules so Libertas was usually shown with a cat or a lion at her feet. At her temple on Mount Aventine, one of Rome's seven hills, the Roman politician Tiberius Gracchus was said to have placed a cat before her statue in tribute.

While freedom should be a right, it is still a privilege in some parts of our modern world. If you are someone who enjoys the liberty to live, work, and worship as you choose (even partaking in the worship of feline deities), never squander the opportunity to use your own self-expression and to fight for that of everyone else. A community working for freedom for all ensures the unique autonomy of each member within it.

MAGICAL CATS

OF CERIDWEN

Ceridwen was the beautiful Celtic goddess of wisdom, the Welsh goddess of poetry, and a white witch practicing healing arts. This powerful sorceress was also a shape-shifter and known as Awen in some Welsh tales. Her mission was to help people, and she often brewed potent elixirs in her cauldron to this end. Ceridwen's two large, magical white cats were her earthly helpers who could sniff out special herbs in the forest needed for her potions and alerted her when dark spirits came near.

Ceridwen was married to Tegid Foel, also a powerful leader, and they had a beautiful daughter named Creirwy. She also had a terribly deformed son named Morfran Afaggdu, whose mind was also afflicted. He later appears in legends of King Arthur. She wanted to help her son and concocted a potent cure for his challenges.

A few drops of Ceridwen's potions had superhuman effects, curing any ailment, and once the intended patient ingested those initial drops, the rest of the liquid became poison. She had an apprentice named Gwion who she left in charge of stirring the pot as it bubbled with enchantments. The boy accidentally got a few drops of liquid (meant to cure her son) onto his hand and licked them off. With that, he became the most beautiful and wise of boys.

Enraged, Ceridwen chased after young Gwion, who was bestowed the many gifts Ceridwen herself had when he ingested the potion. He got the shape-shifting ability and turned into a hare, escaping into the bushes, so Ceridwen became a hound and went after him. Then he became a fish and jumped into a river, so she turned into an otter to pursue him there. When he turned into a bird, she became a hawk. Finally, he turned himself into a single grain of wheat, so she transformed into a chicken and ate him.

When Ceridwen became herself again, the grain had impregnated her and she gave birth to the most magnificent child. This child grew into the famed bard Taliesin, sometimes called Merlin, an advisor to kings and a most powerful druid.

Ceridwen's mythological cats continued in service to her, and friends to Merlin, and they also served as escorts for special souls into the great beyond.

Throughout life, we can have many transformations. Always aspiring for more can ruin what is happening in the present moment. Perhaps by channeling our higher self and reaching out to the Divine Feline Energy that surrounds all beings, we can learn to love who we are in every imperfect moment, and love others with their own imperfections as well.

OVINNIK

In Slavic tales, this mystical being often took the form of a large black cat with blazing yellow eyes, who would hide out in barns and remain unnoticed. If he was discovered, he could bestow either good or bad luck upon the humans who owned the barn and surrounding estate depending on how they reacted to him.

If shooed away, the Ovinnik might burn the barn to the ground. However, the people knew that, if treated with thoughtfulness and kindness and fed, the Ovinnik could be a powerful ally and effective guardian. When he was pleased by the gifts and snacks they left for him, he protected the animals and grain from rodents and scared away evil ghosts.

Ultimately, every being wants to feel safe. Having a place to rest and a full tummy turned this trickster faerie cat into a helpful friend rather than foe. Maybe by being clear about our needs, we can set boundaries to avoid what we don't want and instead get what we desire.

ACKNOWLEDGMENTS

• • • • • • • •

Thank you to Lucy Rose for her incredible illustrations, to my friend and agent Lilly Ghahremani, my wonderful editor Jordana Hawkins, our Production Whiz Amber Morris as well as the entire team at Running Press who brought this project to life.

SOURCES

· · · · · · · · · ·

"A Book of Creatures: Ccoa." *A Book of Creatures*, 27 September 2019, https://abookofcreatures.com/2019/09/27/ccoa.

"Agasou." *Occult World*, https://occult-world.com/agasou.

"Bagheshur—The Tiger God of the Tribes in Central India." *Pugdundee Safaris*, https://www.pugdundeesafaris.com/blog/bagheshur-the -tiger-god-of-the-tribes-in-central-india.

"Carbunclo." *A Book of Creatures*, 17 March 2017, https://abookofcreatures.com/2017/03/17/carbunclo.

"Cat Folklore: Cats Ruled Ancient Rome." *Fully Feline*, 4 February 2013, https://fullyfeline.com/cat-folklore-cats-ruled-ancient-rome.

Davisson, Zack. "The Mystical, Magical, Terrifying Supernatural Cats of Japan." *Zocalo Public Square*, 10 September 2020, https://www.zocalopublicsquare.org/2020/09/10 /supernatural-cats-japan-history-folklore/viewings/glimpses.

Dawsom, Susan. "The Goddess as Cat: From Deity to Demon." *Anthologialitt*, 1 May 2023, https://www.anthologialitt.com/post /the-goddess-as-cat.

"Diana, Roman Religion." *Encyclopaedia Britannica*, 8 March 2024, https://www.britannica.com/topic/Diana-Roman-religion.

Douglas, Andrew. "Naqa, the Ancient City That Was the Kushite Religious Stronghold." *World Atlas*, 7 August 2023, https://www.worldatlas.com/ancient-world/naqa-the-ancient-city -that-was-the-kushite-religious-stronghold.html.

"Ek Balam, a Mayan God Represented by the Black Jaguar." *Yucatan Times*, 20 August 2019, https://www.theyucatantimes.com/2019/08 /ek-balam-a-mayan-god-represented-by-the-black-jaguar.

Evans, Andrew. "The Cats of Kagoshima." *National Geographic*, 11 September 2011, https://www.nationalgeographic.com/travel/article/the-cats-of-kagoshima.

Fields, Kitty. "Cat Goddesses & Male Cat Gods + How to Honor Them." *Other Worldly Oracle*, 26 August 2018, https://otherworldlyoracle.com/cat-goddesses-male-cat-gods.

Friedman, Amy. "The Sacred Cats." *Go Upstate*, 21 September 2005, https://www.goupstate.com/story/news/2005/09/21/the-sacred-cats/29771169007.

Gillespie, Susan D., and Rosemary A. Joyce. "Deity Relationships in Mesoamerican Cosmologies: The Case of the Maya God L." *Ancient Mesoamerica* 9, no. 2 (Fall 1998): 279–296.

"Haetae Korean Mythology: A Fascinating Dive into Korea's Powerful Mythical Creature." *Old World Gods*, https://oldworldgods.com/korean/haetae-mythology.

Hausman, Gerald and Loretta. *The Mythology of Cats*. New York: Berkley Publishing Group, 2000.

Hirst, Kris. "Ix Chel—Mayan Goddess(es) of the Moon, Fertility, and Death." *Thought Co.*, 22 February 2019, https://www.thoughtco.com/ix-chel-mayan-goddess-moon-fertility-death-171592.

Joseph, Charles. "Cats in Islam: From the Quran to the Hadiths." *Cat Checkup*, https://catcheckup.com/cats-in-islam.

Lemaitre, Serge. "Mishipeshu." *The Canadian Encyclopedia*, 4 March 2015, https://www.thecanadianencyclopedia.ca/en/article/mishipeshu.

Lewis, C. S. *The Chronicles of Narnia*. New York: HarperCollins, 2004.

Lewis, Danny. "Each Christmas, Iceland's Yule Cat Takes Fashion Policing to the Extreme." *Smithsonian Magazine*, 19 December 2016, https://www.smithsonianmag.com/smart-news/each-christmas-icelands-yule-cat-takes-fashion-policing-extreme-180961420.

Li, Yang, and Eric Parfitt. "Episode 169: Jinhua Cats." *Chinese Mythology Podcast*, 15 July 2019, https://chinesemythologypodcast.wordpress.com/2019/07/15/episode-169-jinhua-cats.

Luther, Lorre. "7 Cat Gods and Goddesses from Ancient Cultures."
    Catster, 20 February 2024, https://www.catster.com/lifestyle
    /cat-gods-cat-goddesses.

Lynch, Patricia Ann. *African Mythology A to Z*. New York: Facts on File
    Inc., 2010.

"Maahes God of War and Protection." *Cairo Top Tours*, 16 May 2023,
    https://www.cairotoptours.com/Egypt-Travel-Guide/Gods-of
    -Ancient-Egypt/maahes-god-of-war.

Mark, Joshua. "Cats in the Ancient World." *World History*, 17 November
    2012, https://www.worldhistory.org/article/466/cats-in-the-ancient
    -world.

Matthews, Mimi. "Gimalkins, Gothics, & Beware the Cat." *Mimi
    Matthews*, 25 June 2015, https://www.mimimatthews.com
    /2015/06/25/grimalkins-gothics-beware-the-cat.

Meehan, Evan. "Egyptian Goddess Hathor." *Mythopedia*, 29 November
    2022, https://mythopedia.com/topics/hathor.

Mewton, Isaac. "The Role of Cats in Native American Cultures:
    A Historical Insight." *Isaac Mewton,* 28 January 2024,
    https://isaacmewton.net/native-american-cat-significance.

"Moncrif's Cats." *Rodama: A Blog of 18th Century and Revolutionary France*,
    1 November 2016, https://rodama1789.blogspot.com/2016/11
    /moncrifs-cats.html.

"Nergal: The Mesopotamian God of War, Death, and Disease."
    Old World Gods, https://oldworldgods.com/mesopotamian/nergal
    -mesopotamian-god.

"Nunda." *Mythical Creatures*, https://mythical-creatures.com/nunda.

"Old Cat Stories from Around the World." *Messy Beast*,
    http://messybeast.com/moggycat/chinese.htm.

Perinchery, Aathira. "Worshipping Waghoba: Faith Meets
Conversation in Maharashtra Where Humans and Leopards
Share Space." 4 October 2021, https://india.mongabay.com
/2021/10/worshipping-waghoba-faith-meets-conservation
-in-maharashtra-where-humans-and-leopards-share-space.

Pinch, Geraldine. *Handbook of Egyptian Mythology*. Santa Barbara,
CA: ABC-CLIO, 2002.

Qixia, Wang. "The Legend of the Beast Nian." *Confucius Institute*,
https://www.confuciusinstitute.ac.uk/the-legend-of-the-beast
-nian-origins-of-chinese-new-year.

Rafid Kabir, Syed. "Tefnut: Egyptian Goddess of Moisture and Rain."
History Cooperative, 11 March 2024, https://historycooperative.org
/tefnut-goddess-of-moisture-and-rain/.

Ray, Michael. "Galinthias, Greek Mythology." *Encyclopaedia Britannica*,
https://www.britannica.com/topic/Galinthias.

Redish, Laura. "Native American Legends: Lusifee." *Native Languages*,
https://www.native-languages.org/lusifee.htm.

Saunders, Rebecca. "The Fascinating Story Behind the Popular
'Waving Lucky Cat.'" *National Geographic*, 3 May 2021,
https://www.nationalgeographic.com/history/article/the
-fascinating-history-behind-the-popular-waving-lucky-cat.

"Scottish Folklore—Cat Sith & Cu Sith." *Timberbush Tours*, 22 October
2018, https://www.timberbush-tours.co.uk/news-offers/scottish
-folklore-cat-sith-cu-sith.

Shrewsday, Kate. "The Boot-Faced Cat in the Barn." *Kate Shrewsday*,
31 July 2013, https://kateshrewsday.com/2013/07/31/the-boot
-faced-cat-in-the-barn.

"Tepeyollotl." *Aztec Gods and Goddesses*, https://aztecgodsandgoddesses
.weebly.com/tepeyollotl.html.

"The Moche (or Mochica) Culture and Ai Apaec." *The Bojito*, 12 February 2017, https://thebotijo.com/blogs/news/70492741-the-moche-or
-mochica-culture-and-ai-apaec.

Tikkanen, Amy. "Mut Egyptian Goddess." *Encyclopaedia Britannica*,
    25 August 2021, https://www.britannica.com/topic/Mut.

Tolentino, Cierra. "Egyptian Cat Gods: Feline Deities of Ancient Egypt."
    History Cooperative, 2 January 2023, https://historycooperative.org
    /egyptian-cat-gods.

Tolentino, Cierra. "Native American Gods and Goddesses: Deities from
    Different Cultures." *History Cooperative*, 12 October 2022,
    https://historycooperative.org/native-american-gods-and-goddesses.

Twofeathers, Shirley. "African Cat Gods and Lore." *Shirley Twofeathers*,
    24 June 2018, https://shirleytwofeathers.com/The_Blog
    /itsacatastrophe/african-cat-gods-and-lore.

Tyson Smith, Dr. Stuart. "Pylon of the Nubian Lion Temple at Naga."
    Smart History, 8 February 2023, https://smarthistory.org/pylon
    -nubian-lion-temple-naga.

Vocelle, Laura A. *Revered and Reviled: A Complete History of the Domestic Cat*.
    Washington, DC: Great Cat Publications, 2016.

Wilkinson, Richard H. *The Complete Gods and Goddesses of Ancient Egypt*.
    New York: Thames & Hudson, 2003.

Winters, Riley. "The Veneration and Worship of Felines in Ancient
    Egypt." *Ancient Origins*, 9 May 2015, https://www.ancient-origins.net
    /history/veneration-and-worship-felines-ancient-egypt-003030.

Wright, Gregory. "Ceridwen, Celtic Witch." *Mythopedia*, 29 November
    2022, https://mythopedia.com/topics/ceridwen.

Xavier, Cass. "Cat Gods: 7 Feline Deities from Ancient Cultures."
    History Cooperative, 11 March 2024, https://historycooperative.org
    /cat-gods-feline-deities.

Yuko, Elizabeth. "How Cats Became Divine Symbols in Ancient Egypt."
    History, 17 August 2021, https://www.history.com/news/cats-ancient
    -egypt.

ABOUT THE AUTHOR

· · · · · · · ·

Natalie Bovis is a writer, cat mom to five feisty felines, and enthusiast of all things fantastical, historical, and mythological. She has an English mum and French dad but grew up in Santa Fe, New Mexico, a place renowned for its magical energy vortex and a refuge for artists of all kinds. Natalie is an animal advocate, kitten fosterer, and fundraiser for rescues. Her hobbies include hiking, traveling, and vegetarian cooking. Natalie also produces culinary events and vacation retreats in the United States and Europe. She is the author of several mixology books, including *Drinking with My Dog* and *Cocktails with My Cat*. Visit her at TheLiquidMuse.com.

ABOUT THE ILLUSTRATOR

· · · · · · · ·

Lucy Rose is an illustrator and surface pattern designer who graduated from Falmouth University UK with a BA in Illustration. Lucy has always loved print processes, and this is reflected in her work with organic textures and graphic compositions. Currently living by the sea in South Devon, England, she takes inspiration from nature and the botanical elements that surround her.